CAMPAIGN 420

# STOKE FIELD 1487

The Last Battle of the Wars of the Roses

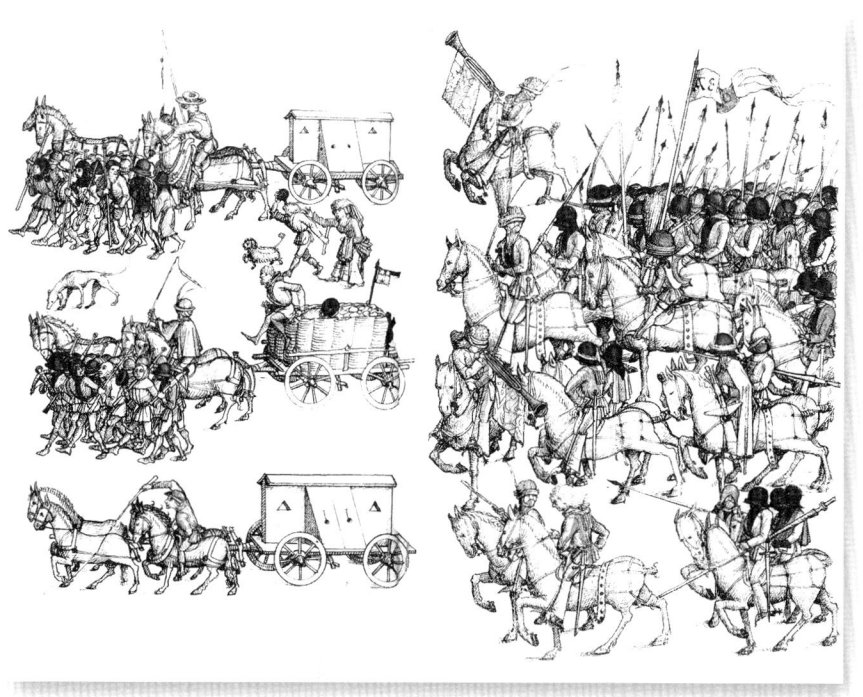

**DICKON WHITEWOOD**  ILLUSTRATED BY GRAHAM TURNER

OSPREY PUBLISHING
Bloomsbury Publishing Plc
Kemp House, Chawley Park, Cumnor Hill, Oxford OX2 9PH, UK
Bloomsbury Publishing Ireland Limited,
29 Earlsfort Terrace, Dublin 2, D02 AY28, Ireland
1385 Broadway, 5th Floor, New York, NY 10018, USA
E-mail: info@ospreypublishing.com
www.ospreypublishing.com

OSPREY is a trademark of Osprey Publishing Ltd

First published in Great Britain in 2025

© Osprey Publishing Ltd, 2025

All rights reserved. No part of this publication may be: i) reproduced or transmitted in any form, electronic or mechanical, including photocopying, recording or by means of any information storage or retrieval system without prior permission in writing from the publishers; or ii) used or reproduced in any way for the training, development or operation of artificial intelligence (AI) technologies, including generative AI technologies. The rights holders expressly reserve this publication from the text and data mining exception as per Article 4(3) of the Digital Single Market Directive (EU) 2019/790

A catalogue record for this book is available from the British Library.

ISBN: PB 9781472867704; eBook 9781472867711; ePDF 9781472867735; XML 9781472867728

25 26 27 28 29   10 9 8 7 6 5 4 3 2 1

Artwork on pp.76–77 © Graham Turner
www.studio88.co.uk
Maps by Bounford.com (map on page 4 is author's collection)
3D BEVs by Paul Kime
Index by Mark Swift
Typeset by PDQ Digital Media Solutions, Bungay, UK
Printed by Repro India Ltd

## Acknowledgements

The author would like to express his sincere thanks to the following individuals for their assistance and courtesy: Kevin Winter, Collections and Learning Officer at the National Civil War Centre in Newark; Keith Dowen, Curator of Arms and Armour at the Wallace Collection; Bob Woosnam-Savage, Curator Emeritus at the Royal Armouries; Caroline Sims, Forensic Osteoarchaeologist; colleagues and friends at English Heritage; staff in the British Library and National Archives; and Brianne Bellio and Alexandra Boulton of Osprey Publishing.

**Artist's Note**
Readers may care to note that the original paintings from which the colour plates in this book were prepared are available for private sale. The Publishers retain all reproduction copyright whatsoever. All enquiries should be addressed to:

Graham Turner, PO Box 568, Aylesbury, Bucks, HP17 8EX, UK
www.studio88.co.uk

The Publishers regret that they cannot enter into any correspondence regarding this matter.

Osprey Publishing supports the Woodland Trust, the UK's leading woodland conservation charity.

To find out more about our authors and books visit **www.ospreypublishing.com**. Here you will find extracts, author interviews, details of forthcoming events and the option to sign up for our newsletter.

For product safety related questions contact productsafety@bloomsbury.com

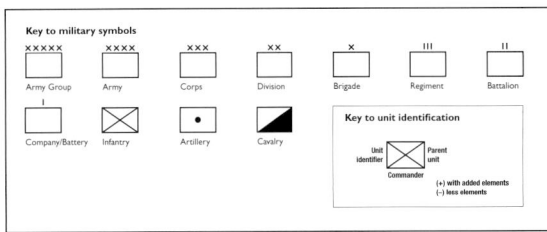

**Front cover main illustration:** The rebel army and Oxford's vanguard come together in fierce hand-to-hand combat. (Graham Turner)
**Title page image:** Detail from the *Medieval House Book of Wolfegg* Castle, *c.*1480, showing an armoured baggage train. (Redrawn from the original by the author)

# CONTENTS

## ORIGINS OF THE CAMPAIGN 5
Bosworth and the Son of Prophecy . The new reign . Stafford and Lovell's rebellion
Lambert Simnel

## CHRONOLOGY 17

## OPPOSING COMMANDERS 19
Henry VII's army . Rebel army

## OPPOSING FORCES 28
Henry VII's army . Rebel army . Numbers

## OPPOSING PLANS 37
Motivations . The Dublin King . 'Keping of ther truthes and due obbeysaunce unto us'
Invasion of England . To Stoke Field

## THE CAMPAIGN 60
The battlefield . Rebel formations . Oxford arrives . The battle . Victory and defeat

## AFTERMATH 86
Punishment and reward . Further plots

## THE BATTLEFIELD TODAY 92

## SELECT BIBLIOGRAPHY 94

## INDEX 95

# Battles of the Wars of the Roses and the main combatants at Stoke Field 1487

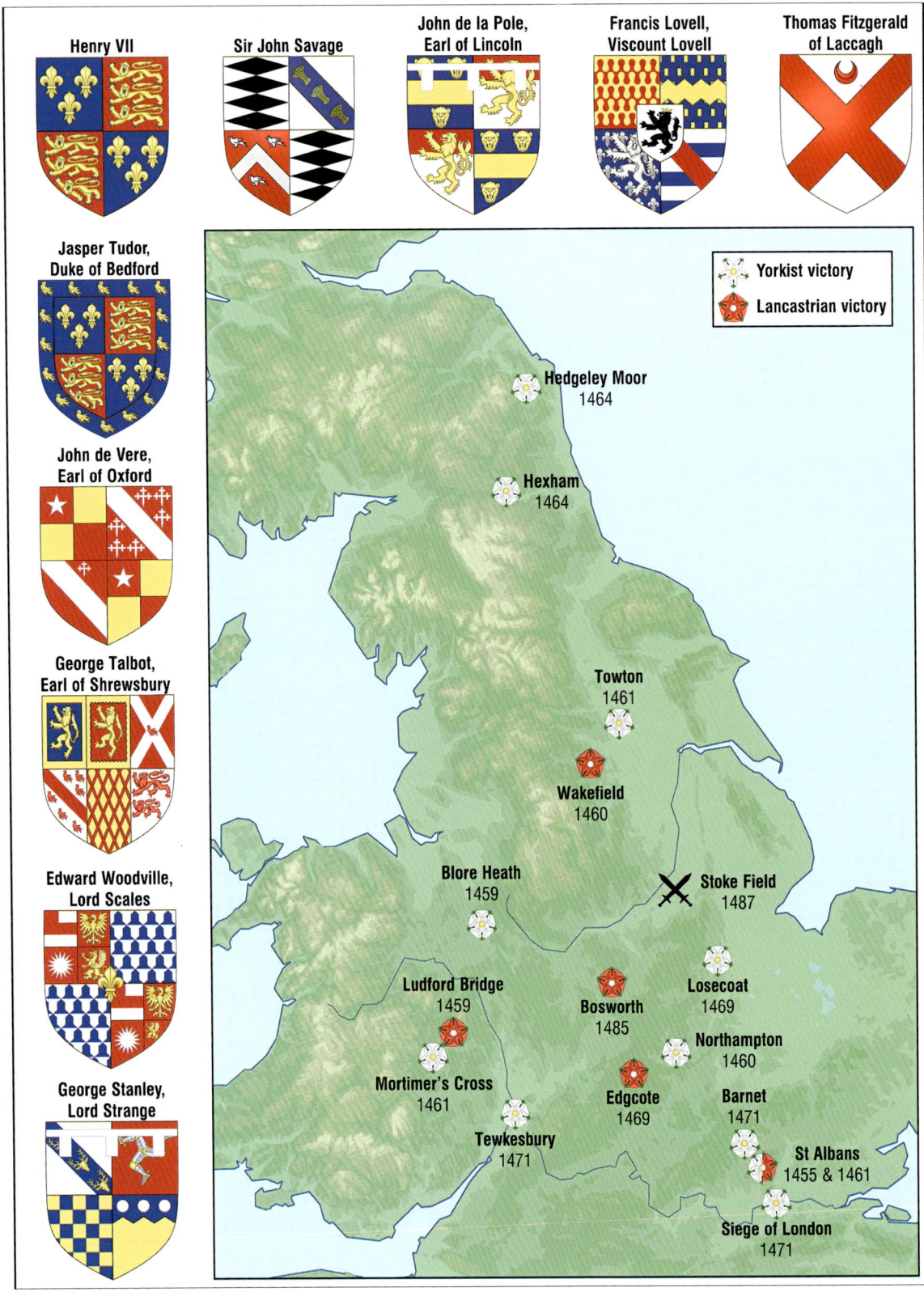

# ORIGINS OF THE CAMPAIGN

## BOSWORTH AND THE SON OF PROPHECY

> Jasper will breed for us a dragon—
> Of the fortunate blood of Brutus is he—
> A Bull of Anglesey to achieve;
> He is the hope of our race.
> (Llanstephan MS. 136, f. 80. National Library of Wales)

During his exile in Brittany, Henry Tudor was identified by the Welsh language poets as the *Mab Darogan* – the Son of Prophecy. Since the subjugation of the country by Edward I, Wales had been ruled by English overlords. The native poets aspired for independence and held that Henry, born in Wales and of noble Welsh lineage, would fulfil prophetic tradition and deliver them from foreign rule through force of arms. To justify his claim to the throne, Henry's ancestry was traced back to heroic figures of English, Scottish and Welsh folklore, such as Arthur, Brutus and Cadwaladr. This flattery of Henry had a serious purpose. The poems deliberately sought to revive long-deferred Welsh hopes and bolster support for the Tudor cause. After the usurpation of Richard III in 1483, the poems became more strident in their call for military action. The *Ode to Saint David* by Dafydd Llwyd contains a rousing line directed at Henry himself: 'England will be reduced under thee … the Boar made cold', an allusion to Richard III's emblem of the white boar and a prediction of the king's death. Llwyd, confident of Henry's forthcoming success, foretold the battle to come: 'Many a nobleman will there be, many their wounds, many a generous duke will suffer pain, many an iron spear and mighty armour; Many a banner shall fall to the ground daily, many a great shout in England.'

This premonition of Henry's victory over Richard at the Battle of Bosworth (1485) and the references to him as a 'dragon' or 'bull' in the poems might

King Henry VII by an unknown Netherlandish artist. The inscription records that the portrait was painted on 29 October 1505, when Henry was 48 years old. (© National Portrait Gallery, London)

seem fanciful. However, to the Welsh and many other contemporaries, there was something miraculous about Henry and his unexpected triumph on the field of battle. The *Croyland Chronicle* reports that in the aftermath of the battle, Henry 'began to be lauded by all men as an angel sent from heaven'.

## THE NEW REIGN

One of Henry's first acts was to date the start of his reign from the day before the battle took place, enabling him to declare Richard and his supporters as traitors. He then sent letters across the kingdom proclaiming his succession and sent Sir Robert Willoughby to Sheriff Hutton to secure the persons of Edward, Earl of Warwick, a potential Yorkist rival, and Princess Elizabeth, eldest daughter of Edward IV, whom he had promised to marry before launching the Bosworth campaign. Henry's coronation took place on 30 October 1485, delayed by an outbreak of sweating sickness, possibly brought into England by Henry's French mercenaries. The rich ceremony took the usual form of consecration, crowning and oath at Westminster Abbey, surrounded by splendid processions and pageantry. A banquet then took place at which Sir Robert Dymoke, the hereditary King's Champion, appeared on horseback to challenge all those who would oppose the new king, just as he had two years previously for Richard III.

One of the issues facing Henry during the early years of his reign was his relative lack of experience in government and administration. This was coupled with the fact that he had little personal knowledge of his kingdom and was a stranger to most of the nobility and people of his realm. His immediate priorities were therefore to reward those who had recently supported him, create his council and appoint qualified men to positions within his government. He was fortunate to be able to draw on the knowledge of several experienced churchmen with proven records of royal administration and personal loyalty to Henry himself. Bishop John Morton, Bishop of Ely, a seasoned royal adviser and enemy of Richard III, was appointed Lord Chancellor. Richard Fox, who had joined Henry's cause in France, became his 'beloved councillor and secretary'. Henry could also count on leading members of the nobility who had fought at Bosworth. His battlefield commander, John de Vere, Earl of Oxford, was richly rewarded with grants of land and positions of office. The Stanley family, whose intervention had proved decisive in Henry's victory, was also rewarded,

A standard of Henry VII featuring the 'Red Dragon of Cadwaladr', a symbol of his descent and legitimacy. (Author's collection)

Sheriff Hutton Castle in Yorkshire was one of the headquarters of the Council of the North, established by Richard III in 1484. Edward, Earl of Warwick, and Princess Elizabeth were taken from here by Henry VII after Bosworth. (Author's collection)

most spectacularly through the elevation of Thomas Stanley, Henry's stepfather, to the peerage as Earl of Derby in October 1485. Together, such men compensated for Henry's inexperience in English customs and ensured the new government had a competent and effective administration. Most highly regarded and favoured by Henry were his mother Margaret Beaufort and uncle Jasper Tudor, his longest and most trusted supporters. Both took on active roles within Henry's innermost councils. Other associates known since his childhood, such as Sir Reginald Bray, were similarly held in high regard and rewarded accordingly.

Many other supporters of less elevated rank were promoted in ways that ensured that power passed to people on whom Henry could rely. Ricardian adherents were replaced as constables of castles and in other prominent local roles, quietly ensuring that the power of the new government was extended throughout the country. Henry remained cautious, however, about his personal security and soon decided to form a personal bodyguard of 50–200 men, known as the Yeoman of the Guard.

After the coronation, Henry opened his first parliament, which was necessary to organize the royal finances, lawfully reward his supporters, punish his enemies and provide the new reign with the formal basis of legitimate authority. The attainders previously passed against Henry and his followers were reversed and new attainders were passed against Richard III and those who had fought with him at Bosworth. In general, however, the new king was inclined to be lenient to those willing to accept his rule. Henry Percy, Earl of Northumberland, who had failed to engage on Richard's behalf at Bosworth, was soon released from imprisonment. Thomas Howard, Earl of Surrey, was pardoned in March 1486 and soon gained office in the north. Perhaps most surprising was the treatment of John de la Pole, Earl of Lincoln, Richard III's nephew. Even though he was considered as a plausible Yorkist heir and may even have fought against Henry at Bosworth, Lincoln seems not to have been attainted or imprisoned, instead being treated honourably and included in the new king's councils.

A portrait of Elizabeth of York by an unknown artist. It shows her at 34 years of age and is first recorded as hanging at Whitehall Palace in 1542. (The Royal Collection)

# Henry VII's progress after Bosworth and the rebellion of 1486

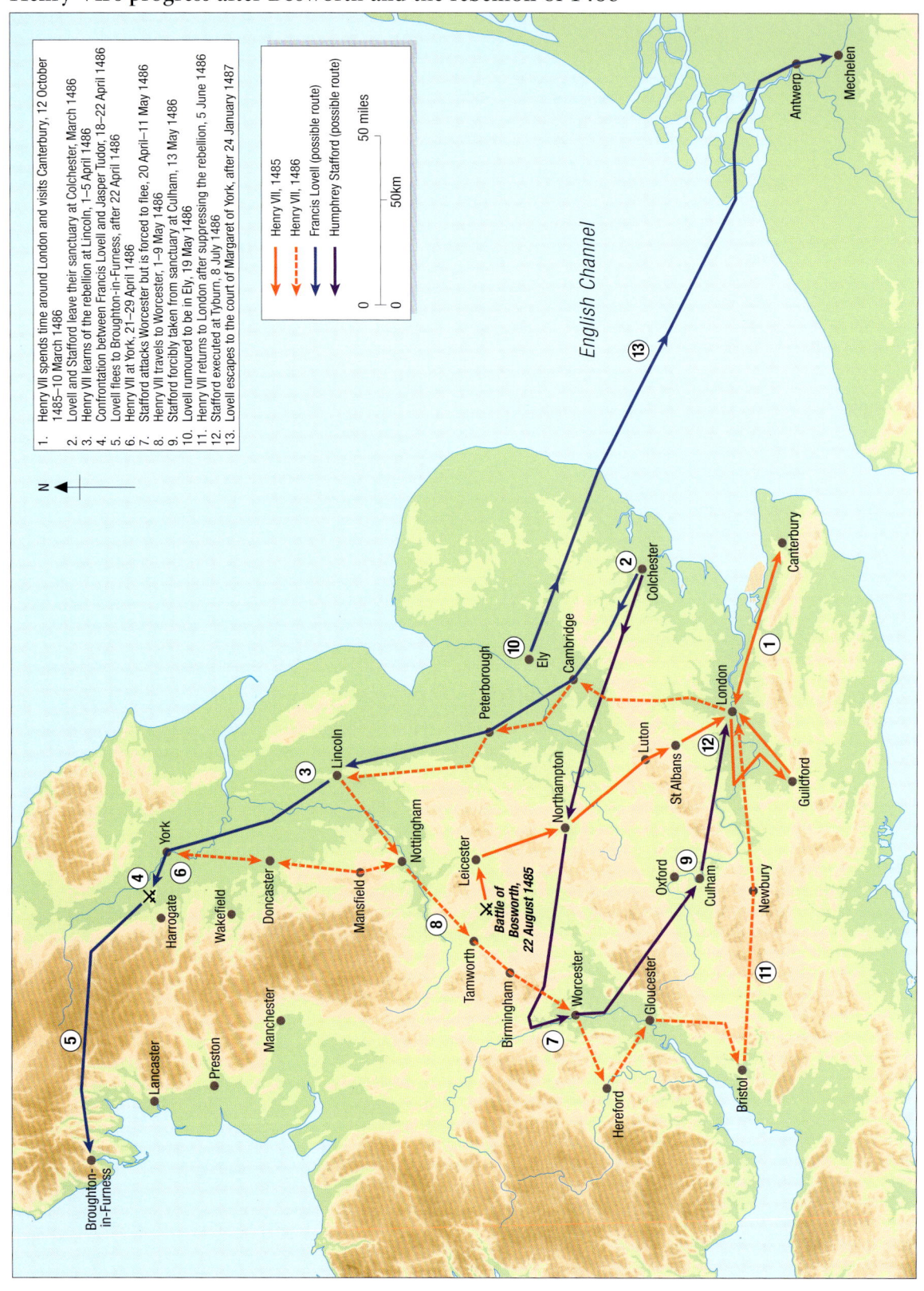

After matters of finance and public peace had been discussed, parliament urged the king to take Princess Elizabeth as his wife, as Henry had previously pledged. Henry accepted and the wedding took place on 18 January 1486, uniting the Houses of York and Lancaster. On 27 March, the union was enhanced when Pope Innocent VIII issued a dispensation for the marriage, recognized the legitimacy of Henry's title to the English throne and threatened the excommunication of any person who disputed it. Unfortunately for Henry, it was soon demonstrated that papal support was insufficient to prevent some Ricardian die-hards from taking up arms against him.

Henry's primary issue was that there were many people whose sympathies and hopes of preferment rested on a restored Yorkist regime. There was no shortage of potential Yorkist claimants, and not all those who might support them had perished at Bosworth. Henry also needed to establish his position abroad by forging diplomatic relations with foreign countries, most importantly France and Scotland, but also with his own subjects in Ireland. Each of these had their political interests, not all of which aligned with Henry's own. Most dangerously, a significant threat came from the Low Countries through the personal enmity of its governor, Margaret of York, Duchess of Burgundy, a sister to the Yorkist kings Edward IV and Richard III. Henry, whose recent invasion had been possible only because of the support he had received from Charles VIII of France, must have been highly aware of the dangers that could threaten him from abroad.

## STAFFORD AND LOVELL'S REBELLION

After his coronation, Henry faced a need to show himself to his people around the country, ensure their loyalty and receive their homage. Although southern England had largely supported him, the affiliation of other parts of the country, in particular the north, was less certain. York had well-known sympathies for Richard III as a result of the favour he had shown the city. Sir Roger Cotam, who had been sent by Henry to proclaim the new king after Bosworth, reported that he 'durst not for fere of deth come trugh the Citie to speake with the Maire and his Brethre' – justifiably, for only the day before Cotam's arrival, the mayor and aldermen of York had registered their sorrow for the late and lawful King Richard 'pitiously slane and murderd, to the grete hevyness of this Citie'. Several months later, Richard was still remembered as 'the moost famous prince of blessed memory, King Richard, late decesid'. In another act of defiance, Miles Metcalfe, one of the few men Henry exempted from a general pardon issued after Bosworth, continued in his role of city recorder despite a letter sent by Henry in early October calling him seditious and unfit for office. The Tudor court historian, Polydore Vergil, says that as a result of these acts of defiance, one of Henry's principal desires was to 'reduce to obedience Yorkshire, which had particularly supported the opposing factions'.

Henry set out on his first progress on 10 March 1486, reaching Lincoln on 20 March. There he attended Easter festivities in the cathedral and observed the ancient customs of distributing alms and washing the feet of the poor. In early April, however, while still in the city, Henry received reports of the first challenge to his reign. Sir Humphrey Stafford of Grafton, his brother Thomas, and Francis Lovell, Viscount Lovell, who had all survived

Bosworth and been attainted in Henry's first parliament, had broken sanctuary at Colchester with the intention of raising a rebellion. According to the testimony of Sir Hugh Conway, who broke the news to the king, Henry listened to the report in some disbelief and 'said that hyt could not be so, and resoned with me alweyes to the contrary of my said sayynges'. Whether he was genuinely taken by surprise or not, Henry immediately took precautions and sent riders to look for the rebels, including Thomas Cokesey, who wrote to Bishop Morton soon after to inform him of his efforts. The *Croyland Chronicle* says that Henry had around him 'a great multitude of men, but all of them unarmed', suggesting the rebellion was indeed unexpected.

Henry nevertheless continued his progress to York. A firsthand account of the journey, printed in Leland's *Collectanea*, says that Henry's retinue grew as he approached the city so that it included bishops, earls, lords, knights and a 'merveolous great nombre [on] so short a warnyng of esquiers, gentilmen, and yomen in defencible array'. Henry also conducted himself in a way calculated to impress his confidence and royal status, dressed in ermine and cloth of gold. On his arrival into the city, the *York House Book* records that Henry received worrying news that Francis Lovell and 'certeynes rebelles aboute Rypon and Midlem [Middleham]' had assembled a large force intent on threatening York. Vergil says that this caused Henry to be fearful due to the absence of his full army and the doubtful allegiance of the city. However, it is clear from the firsthand account that the city authorities had made conspicuous efforts to welcome and entertain the king with pageants and performances, knowing he expected to receive suitable gestures of their loyalty. Henry was also immediately able to send 3,000 men, a significant armed force, against Lovell under the command of Jasper Tudor. Edward Hall mentions an interesting detail that many of these men were 'not strongly armed to do a great enterpryce for their brest plates for the moost part were made of tanned lether'.

The Garter plate of Francis Lovell, installed in 1483 in the Chapel of St George, Windsor. The silver helm above the shield is surmounted by the crest of a silver dog with a gold crown and chain around his neck, his personal emblem. (Author's collection)

Although Henry may not have been fully prepared, the uprising was nonetheless a failure. Jasper Tudor met the rebels one or two days later to the north-west of York. Approaching the enemy encampment, Tudor consulted with his captains, perhaps including Northumberland, whom the *Croyland Chronicle* credits with foiling 'a stratagem on part of the enemy'. To avoid battle, the heralds were sent to the rebel position and proclaimed that anyone who laid down their arms would be granted pardon. This caused Lovell, 'either not trusting in himself or terrified', to flee from the rebel camp during the night. The remaining rebels quickly begged for mercy, although *Croyland*'s note that those who had prompted the movement were hanged on the gallows suggests that several ringleaders were singled out for punishment. Lovell fled into hiding among the Furness Fells of Lancashire. Initially, he sought sanctuary at Furness Abbey, but he was forced to move on when a monk recognized him on account of a large mastiff that habitually accompanied him.

The castle of Middleham in Wensleydale, Yorkshire. Commonly said to be the 'childhood home' of Richard III, it was certainly the birthplace of his son, Edward, in about 1474. Lovell raised his rebellion of 1486 in the district, and a year later, it would again play a role during the Stoke campaign. (Author's collection)

He then moved to Broughton Hall, where he was welcomed by the Yorkist adherent, Sir Thomas Broughton. After some time in the north, Lovell seems to have journeyed south and, on 19 May, the Countess of Oxford wrote to John Paston with information that he was in Ely. From there, Lovell went across the sea sometime after 24 January 1487 with '14 persons and no more'. His destination was the Low Countries and the court of Margaret of York, with whom, according to Vergil, he discussed further, more ambitious plans for rebellion.

One mystery surrounding the events in York is the confession of a certain James Taite in May 1487. He claimed that while Lincoln was in York with the king, two men from Middleham had dined in the earl's household and that he had considered going 'over the walls' to join one 'Robyn of Redesdale'. This was presumably a leader among the rebels, possibly even Lovell himself, operating under a false identity. The same name had been used in 1469 during two rebellions against Edward IV and its reappearance seems to have been consciously designed to echo these previous events.

A possibility also exists that the rebellion included a plot to murder the king. In his reference to the actions of Northumberland, the *Croyland Chronicle* says that the earl averted disaster when the king was 'intent upon his devotions' on the feast of St George (23 April) and was 'nearly slain'. Although this may be a reference to the wider plot, the detail of Henry being at prayer suggests a more specific and nefarious action targeted against the king's person. Given Taite's confession, it is possible that Lincoln was a co-conspirator. If so, the earl hid his involvement successfully and no suspicion seems to have been cast on him.

With the defeat of Lovell, the king moved south to deal with the second outbreak of rebellion. After leaving Colchester, Humphrey Stafford and his brother Thomas had made their way to Worcestershire, their home county. Stafford's first action was at Bromsgrove, next to his home at Grafton Manor, where he deceived the townsfolk into his

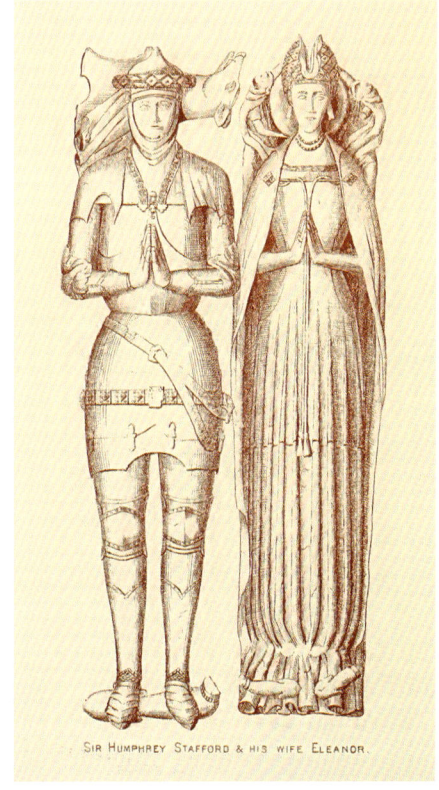

The effigies of Humphrey Stafford's parents in St John's Church, Bromsgrove. The monument depicts Stafford's father wearing the Lancastrian 'SS' collar, demonstrating how family loyalties could shift during the Wars of the Roses. (Author's collection)

support by producing forged letters patent stating Henry VII had pardoned him. He then proceeded to Kidderminster, where he had arranged to meet many of his closest adherents. His immediate plan centred on seizing Worcester, which was partially achieved when his men broke in and held the gates. Stafford's control of the city, however, was short lived and he was forced to retreat to a wood several miles away, near Bewdley. The bailiff and commonality of Worcester were later indicted for allowing the rebels to enter the city due to their negligence in not providing a suitable guard.

Stafford's support melted away with news of Lovell's failure and the king's movement south. Thomas Cokesey led a raid on the rebel camp with 400 men, but found it deserted. Humphrey and Thomas had already fled to sanctuary at Culham, Oxfordshire, halting only to steal horses at Upton-on-Severn. At Nottingham, Henry appointed commissioners, including Lincoln, the Duke of Bedford, and the earls of Oxford and Derby, to investigate the various treasons and felonies that had been committed. On 13 May, Humphrey Stafford was forcibly taken from sanctuary by Sir John Savage and around 50 of his men, in clear violation of the privileges of the church. This later gave rise to a *cause célèbre* when Stafford was tried in King's Bench. Although the violation of sanctuary caused legal difficulties, it was judged that this recourse was not pleadable in cases of treason. Stafford was condemned to a traitor's death and executed at Tyburn. His brother Thomas was more fortunate and received a reprieve.

Stafford and Lovell's objective appears to have been to raise men in their respective areas and then combine their forces. It is possible their plan included a conspiracy to murder the king in a city they felt to be favourable to the endeavour. Their ultimate ambition may be indicated by the fact that some of the rebels were later indicted for shouting 'A Warwyke, A Warwyke!', a rallying cry showing their support for the imprisoned Earl of Warwick. During the rebellion, rumours were spread that he had been set free on the Isle of Guernsey and had joined Lovell in the north. On 2 May, there was an uprising in London, probably co-ordinated with the other outbreaks, during which malcontents raised Warwick's standard of the ragged staff.

With the rebellion crushed, Henry VII journeyed back to London. Some months later, on 19 September 1486, the queen bore a son who combined the blood of both royal houses, Lancaster and York. Born in Winchester, Britain's ancient capital, and given the legendary name of Arthur, his christening was attended by many of the leading nobility in what was intended by the new government to be a celebration of newfound unity symbolized by his birth.

There is no record of how Lovell spent the months before his flight to the Continent, but his efforts against Henry VII certainly continued. He was probably aided by John Sante, Abbot of Abingdon, a devoted Yorkist whose career had been advanced by Edward IV. Sante would have been well known to Lovell due to their shared religious and financial interests in Abingdon and the proximity of the town to Lovell's principal manors, Minster Lovell and Greys Court. Sante played a small part in the rebellion of 1486 when

The bear and ragged staff was the heraldic emblem and badge of the earls of Warwick. Heraldry associated with Warwick was used by both Yorkists and Lancastrians in the period 1485–87. (Author's collection)

Humphrey Stafford sought sanctuary at the abbey's property at Culham. He later appeared in court to complain about the violation of his abbey's rights. All this action achieved, however, was a fine from Henry VII for harbouring Stafford, which added considerably to Sante's resentment. His subsequent involvement in plots against Henry is heavily implied by his prosecution in 1489 for 'falsly and traiterously compassyng, conspiryng and ymagynyng the destruction of the Kyng', specifically for sending money and other assistance two years earlier to Lincoln, who was then at the court of Margaret of York. Sante's other connections included the University of Oxford, where the next serious threat to Henry VII emerged, revolving around a boy known to history as Lambert Simnel.

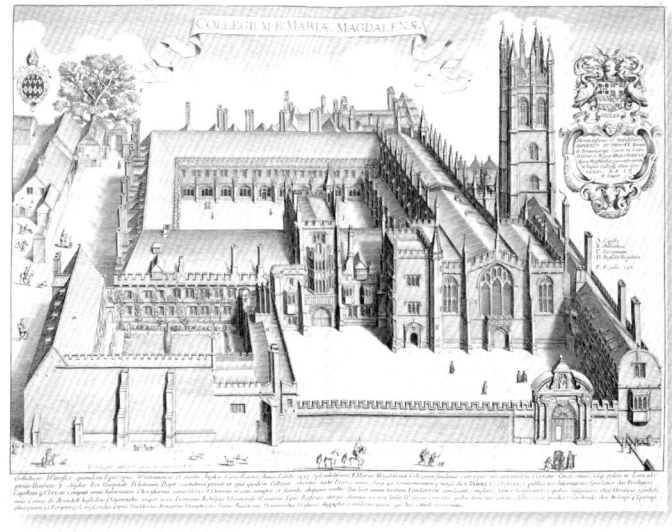

Magdalen College from David Loggan's *Oxonia Illustrata*, published in 1675. Magdalen hosted Richard III on two occasions and may later have been connected to the Simnel plot. (Author's collection)

## LAMBERT SIMNEL

Vergil's 'official' account states that Richard Simons, a scholar-priest of Oxford, hatched a scheme to train a boy to impersonate a prince of the House of York. Simons' purpose, according to Vergil, was to make the boy king and secure his own promotion to primate of England. For the impersonation, he selected Lambert Simnel, who was roughly the correct age and possessed the required good looks, and schooled him in letters, the goodly arts, royal manners and pedigree, so that 'when the need should arise, the common people might admire the boy's character and more readily believe the lie'. The Earl of Warwick was chosen as the subject for the impersonation when Simons heard a rumour that the real Warwick had died in the Tower. He then took the impostor to Ireland to meet with members of the Irish peerage, whom Simons had heard were disaffected with Henry VII. His arguments and the boy's performance convinced them he was genuine, particularly the Irish Chancellor, Thomas FitzGerald, who was 'especially deceived by this show of truth and offered the boy his hospitality'. To secure more support, messengers were sent to old followers of Richard III asking for their assistance, while other messengers were sent to Margaret of York. Vergil says that, although she regarded the business as fraudulent, Margaret promised to give her aid and recruit greater support for the conspiracy.

This version of events is born out to some degree by other evidence. On 17 February 1487, the Register of the Archbishop of Canterbury says that a priest called William Simons was brought before John Morton (enthroned as archbishop in January 1487) and confessed to having organized the plot late the previous year and then taken Simnel, the lowborn son of an organ maker from Oxford, to Ireland. Simons had then apparently crossed the sea to speak with Lovell in the Furness Fells, only to be captured. As early as November 1487, the act of attainder passed against the defeated at Stoke gives the name of the impostor as Lambert Simnel and says that he was the son of a joiner.

This accords with evidence of known inhabitants of Oxford in the late 15th century. A man called Thomas Simnel is recorded as living in Oxford in the late 1470s and held a tenement next to William Wooton, an organ builder, suggesting that Thomas may have been in a similar woodworking trade. Thomas' surname indicates that he was probably Flemish, and it is possible that he could have named his son after St Lambert of Maastricht, whose relics had recently been re-housed at great expense by Margaret of York's husband, Charles the Bold, Duke of Burgundy.

However, there are considerable gaps in Vergil's account and conflicting evidence also exists which casts doubt on the traditionally accepted version of events. Most obviously, Vergil himself was a court historian whose account heavily favoured Henry VII and omitted any compromising or unsympathetic detail. Much uncertainty is also caused by Vergil's lack of a timeline for the events he describes, which makes it difficult to place them in a timeframe alongside other known events. It is also unclear how Simons – named alternatively William or Richard in the sources (although a possibility exists that they were brothers) – can have had enough experience of the royal court to tutor his pupil adequately, or that he would be brazen enough to hatch the scheme without support from a patron. Furthermore, there is no certainty that Thomas Simnel had a son, and the unusual and foreign-sounding name of Lambert Simnel appears custom-made to have provoked derision, exactly as Henry VII and his government might have desired if they had fabricated the name to ridicule the claimant and present him as an obvious impostor. It is therefore highly curious that a herald's account of the battle (hereafter referred to as the *Herald's Report*), written by an eyewitness only a few years after the events, says that the boy captured at Stoke Field 'was indeed called John'. The name of 'John' was corrected to 'Lambert' by the antiquarian John Leland in his subsequent transcript of the account, compiled around 50 years later. By this point, the 'official' version had gained wide acceptance, and it is likely Leland thought he was simply correcting the herald's mistake.

The tomb effigy of John Morton near the altar of the Virgin Mary in the Chapel of Our Lady Undercroft, Canterbury Cathedral. (Author's collection)

There is also confusion among contemporary sources about whether the impostor claimed to be Warwick or one of Edward IV's sons, Edward V and Richard, Duke of York (commonly known as the Princes in the Tower after their confinement there during the reign of Richard III). The accounts of several continental authors, such as Jean Molinet, Adrian de Budt and Caspar Weinrich, provide no indication the claimant was an impostor, simply calling him Warwick or 'the son of Clarence'. This possibly reflects the rumour that his father, George, Duke of Clarence, was said to have attempted to send his son to Ireland before his arrest and execution in 1478. Bernard André's account says that the impostor was the son of a miller or cobbler who pretended to be one of the sons of Edward IV. A similar story can be found in the *Annals of Ulster*, which says that the boy in Ireland was the 'son of the Duke of York', perhaps meaning Richard, Duke of York. Some evidence of contemporary confusion is even provided by Vergil, who admits that there were rumours that the Princes in the Tower had survived and that Simons considered one of them as the subject for the impersonation before settling on Warwick. In 1526 the idea that the impostor claimed to be a son of Edward IV persisted, and among the *Letters and Papers, Foreign and Domestic of Henry VIII* a note on Ireland talks of Simnel as 'an organ-maker's son, named one of king Edward's sons'. A receipt dated 16 December 1487, discovered recently in the Archives de Nord in Lille, records the payment of 120 livres for 400 long pikes. The purpose given is that they were 'to serve her [Margaret of York's] nephew – son of King Edward, late her brother (may god save his soul), [who was] expelled from his dominion'. Although this receipt does not prove that Edward V had survived, as has been claimed, it does provide plausible evidence that Margaret believed, or feigned to believe, the boy to be Edward V.

That there was initial uncertainty in Henry VII's court over the boy's identity is suggested by his subsequent actions. Rumours of a pretender in Ireland had probably become common by November 1486, and in some quarters, the belief seems to have been that it was Warwick. On the 29th, Thomas Betanson wrote to his master Sir Robert Plumpton, 'Also hereis but litle spech … of the Earle of Warwick now, but after Christenmas they say thur wylbe more spech of'. According to Bernard André, Henry was disturbed enough by the rumours to send a herald to Ireland to appraise the boy, who returned disturbingly impressed with the boy's prompt answers to the questions directed at him. That there is some truth to this story is suggested by a royal account payment in March 1487 to John Yonge, Falcon pursuivant, for 'his secret business' in Ireland.

In early February, Henry convened his council to discuss what should be done. Then, on 19 February, the 'real' Warwick was taken from the Tower and paraded through the streets to St Paul's, and appeared to the crowds standing in front of Archbishop John Morton so that all could see him. Henry also began to move against those suspected of treachery. In Devon and Cornwall, Richard Edgcumbe was given the power to arrest two men suspected of disloyalty, Henry Bodrugan and John Beaumont, although both escaped capture and fled to Ireland. Bishop Robert Stillington, who was an associate of Clarence and whose indiscretion regarding Edward IV's allegedly bigamous marriage had paved Richard III's route to the throne, was arrested and taken to Windsor to be questioned. At the same time, Henry had his mother-in-law Elizabeth Woodville (Edward IV's wife and queen) confined to the nunnery at Bermondsey, and control of her finances transferred to her daughter, Queen Elizabeth. Although there is evidence Woodville had already considered entering seclusion voluntarily, the timing of this action is suspicious, especially when coupled with the imprisonment of her son, Thomas Grey, Marquess of Dorset, soon after. The king is supposed to have remarked that 'if he [Thomas] were a friend … he would scarcely take amiss this small indignity for the sake of his own safety; or, if he were an enemy, lest he work harm'.

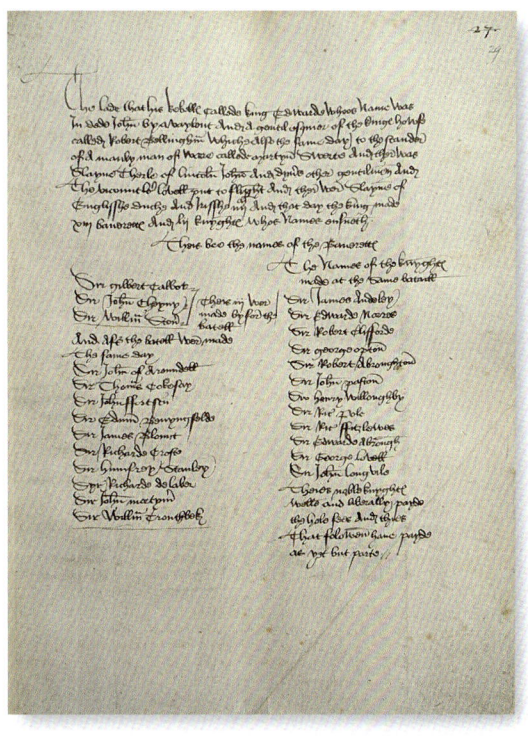

The *Herald's Report* in British Library Cotton MS Julius BXII, f. 29r. This first-hand account, written by an anonymous herald, contains a description of the battle in which it says the boy captured 'whoos name was in dede John' was an impostor. This is followed by a list of those knighted by Henry VII. (From the British Library Collection: Julius BXII, f. 29r)

Although Stillington might have been expected to support Warwick's claim, it is harder to see what advantage the Woodvilles would derive from Henry VII's replacement by Warwick, especially after the birth of Prince Arthur, their close relation. However, if there were rumours about the survival of the Princes in the Tower and the supposed presence of at least one of them in Ireland, it is much easier to see why Henry VII would suspect their loyalty. There is good reason therefore to suppose that many people were unsure about the real identity of the claimant at the outbreak of the rebellion. Henry accordingly took what action he could to identify him, discredit the rumours and secure control of those he felt might be disloyal.

If there is ambiguity about who the pretender claimed or was believed to be, there is also a persistent mystery about his true identity. However plausible the Tudor version of him being the son of a tradesman in Oxford may be, there has been no shortage of theories both contemporary and subsequently which have suggested he was otherwise. There is certainly a danger of reading Vergil's account uncritically without allowing for other possibilities. However, the arguments supporting the idea that the impostor was a true prince of York – such as Edward V, Richard, Duke of York, or the 'real' Warwick smuggled out of imprisonment – cannot be advanced with any greater degree of certainty than the 'official' version favouring a deliberate fraud planted to impersonate one of them. Whatever the truth of the boy's identity, the government did not take long to decide what story they would propagate. As early as July 1487, Henry VII wrote to the Pope to say that the impostor had pretended to be the son of Clarence. A few months later, the impostor had been publicly named as Lambert Simnel.

As with the events of 1486, the Earl of Lincoln's part in the Lambert Simnel affair is unknown, as is the extent of his communications with Lovell or any of the other suspected conspirators. According to Vergil, Lincoln's decision to rebel against Henry VII was a sudden decision made in reaction to the news of Lambert Simnel's acclamation in Ireland, with the earl concluding 'that this opportunity for rebellion was in no wise to be ignored, and that the Irish enterprises were to be supported by all means, less they come to naught'. That he may have been involved in the conspiracy earlier is suggested by James Taite's confession, who said that he had met agents of Lincoln at Doncaster, disguised as merchants, taking a white horse north with saddle-bags full of gold and silver, with a plan to meet the prior of Tynemouth, Sir Thomas Mauleverer, and others. The same men had boasted that Lincoln would give his enemies 'a brekefast that oweth hyme noo luff nor favour'. In December 1486 or January 1487, Lincoln is known to have borrowed £20 from the foundation at Ewelme, perhaps some of the money sent abroad by Abbot Sante. If so, this suggests he had been preparing his next action for some time.

Lincoln was present at the events in London in February and was with the king at Sheen in early March, where he 'daily spoke' with Warwick while the boy remained outside the Tower. There is no evidence that Henry had any suspicions of Lincoln's disloyalty. It must therefore have come as a deep surprise when, on 9 March, Lincoln abruptly departed from court and sailed to Flanders and his aunt Margaret of York.

Margaret of Burgundy by an unknown artist. Married to Duke Charles the Bold in 1468 to secure an alliance between England and Burgundy, she acted as protector after Charles' death in 1477 and became a focal point of resistance against Henry VII. (RMN-Grand Palais/Jean-Gilles Berizzi/Dist. Photo SCALA, Florence)

# CHRONOLOGY

| | | |
|---|---|---|
| 1457 | 28 January | Birth of Henry Tudor in Pembroke Castle |
| c.1460 | unknown | Birth of John de la Pole |
| 1461 | 4 March | Accession of Edward IV |
| | 29 March | Battle of Towton |
| 1467 | 13 March | John de la Pole created Earl of Lincoln |
| 1470 | 3 October | Restoration (known as the Readeption) of Henry VI |
| 1471 | 14 April | Battle of Barnet and death of Warwick 'The Kingmaker' |
| | 4 May | Battle of Tewkesbury |
| | 21 May | Death of Henry VI |
| | 2 June | Jasper and Henry Tudor escape from Tenby to Brittany |
| 1474 | 29 July | Beginning of the siege of Neuss |
| 1483 | 9 April | Death of Edward IV and accession of Edward V |
| | 26 June | Accession of Richard III |
| | 11 October | Richard learns of a revolt in southern England |
| | 30 October | Henry Tudor launches expedition from Brittany |
| | 2 November | Execution of the Duke of Buckingham |
| | 25 December | Oath of Henry Tudor at Rennes to marry Elizabeth of York |
| 1484 | 9 April | Death of Edward of Middleham |
| | 21 August | Lincoln made lieutenant of Ireland |
| | Summer | Lincoln made president of the council in the north |
| 1485 | 1 August | Henry Tudor sails from Harfleur |
| | 7 August | Henry Tudor lands near Milford Haven |
| | 22 August | Battle of Bosworth and death of Richard III |
| | 30 October | Henry VII crowned |
| 1486 | 18 January | Henry VII marries Elizabeth of York |
| | Easter period | Rebellion of Lovell and the Staffords |
| | 3 May | Lincoln leads the inquiry into Stafford's treason |
| | 13 May | Humphrey Stafford forcibly taken from sanctuary |
| | 19 September | Birth of Prince Arthur |
| 1487 | 9 March | Lincoln flees to the Low Countries |
| | 27 May | Coronation of Lambert Simnel as Edward VI in Dublin |
| | 4 June | Simnel and the rebels land at Furness |
| | 10 June | Skirmish at Bramham Moor, near Tadcaster |
| | 12 June | Bootham Bar attacked by the Scropes |
| | 12–13 June | Skirmish between the rebels and Lord Scales near Doncaster |
| | 16 June | Battle of Stoke Field |
| | 25 November | Coronation of Queen Elizabeth |
| 1489 | 28 April | Earl of Northumberland killed |
| 1491 | 28 June | Birth of Prince Henry (later Henry VIII) |
| | November | Perkin Warbeck proclaimed as Richard, Duke of York |
| 1492 | | Warbeck in France and Burgundy |
| 1493 | November | Warbeck with Maximilian in Vienna |
| 1495 | 16 February | Execution of Sir William Stanley |
| | 23 July to 3 August | Warbeck's failure in Kent |
| | November | Warbeck arrives in Scotland |

| 1496 | September | Invasion by the Scots and Warbeck into England |
| 1497 | 17 June | Cornish uprising beaten at Blackheath |
| | 7 September | Warbeck lands in Cornwall |
| | 5 October | Warbeck surrenders to Henry VII |
| 1499 | 12 February | Execution of Ralph Wilford (imposter) |
| | 23 November | Execution of Warbeck |
| | 28 November | Execution of Edward, Earl of Warwick |
| 1502 | 2 April | Death of Prince Arthur, Prince of Wales |
| 1509 | 21 April | Death of Henry VII |

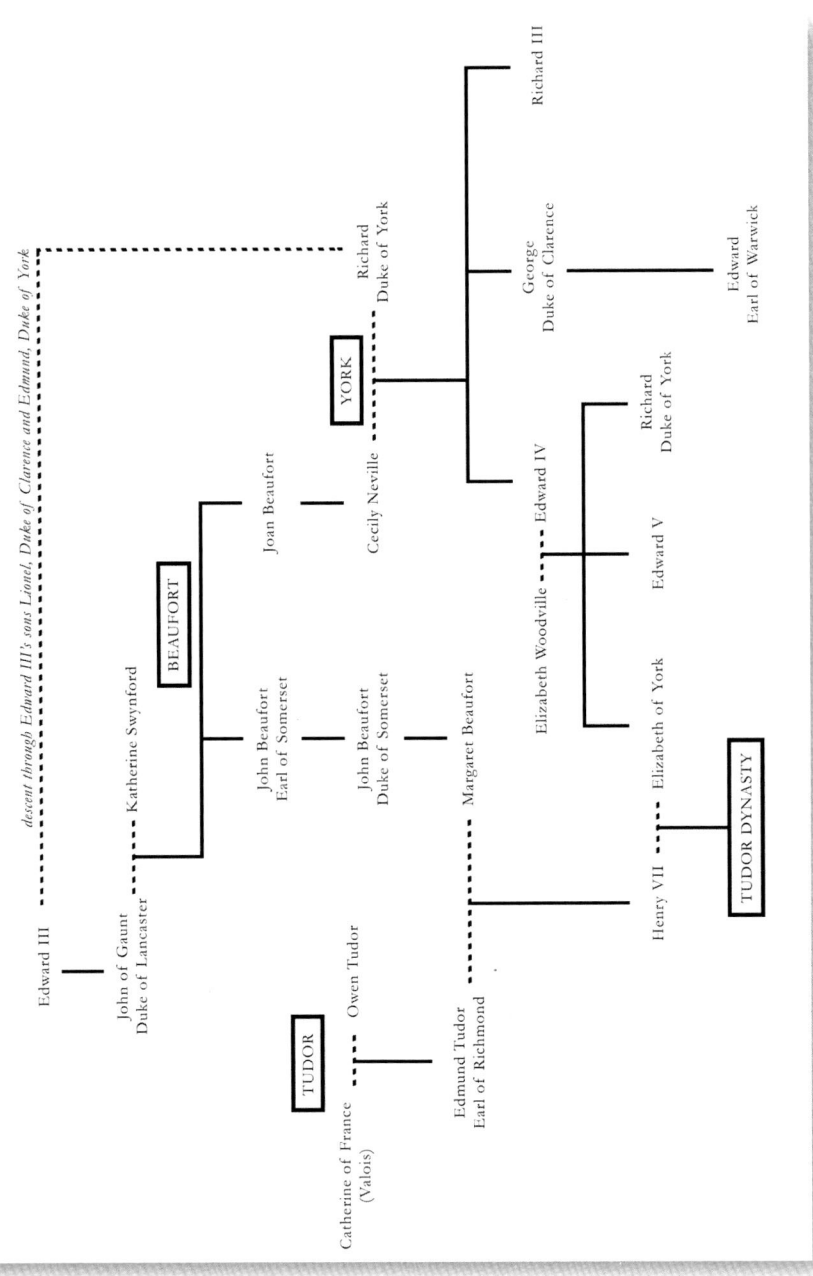

Simplified genealogical tree showing the lineage and relationships between the Houses of Plantagenet, York, Beaufort and Tudor. (Author's collection)

# OPPOSING COMMANDERS

## HENRY VII'S ARMY

**Henry VII** was born on 28 January 1457 at Pembroke Castle. His father, Edmund Tudor, Earl of Richmond, died in November 1456, two months before Henry's birth, probably from plague. His mother, Margaret Beaufort, was only 13 at the time of Henry's birth and seems to have suffered severely during the delivery, and certainly did not bear any more children. Despite these inauspicious beginnings, the child's wardship was potentially lucrative and, in 1462, Edward IV granted it to William Herbert, Earl of Pembroke, his principal Welsh supporter. Intended by Herbert as a marriage partner for his daughter Maud, Henry spent his early years at Raglan Castle, tutored in gentlemanly and warlike pursuits. Bernard André reported that one of his tutors, Andreas Scotus, said that 'he had never heard of children capable of learning with such quickness at that age', suggesting that Henry soon began to demonstrate the intelligence for which he later became well known. He was visited only occasionally at this time by his mother, who in 1458 had married her kinsman Henry Stafford, but she retained a keen interest in Henry's upbringing and the two seem to have written to each other regularly.

In 1469, Herbert was executed following his defeat at the Battle of Edgcote and for the next 15 months, Henry lived at Weobley, Herefordshire, with Herbert's widow. In October 1470, during the Readeption of Henry VI, Henry and his mother visited the king, who is said by early Tudor propaganda to have foretold Henry's future reign.

Edward IV's victories at Barnet and Tewksbury in April and May 1471, together with the deaths of Henry VI and his son, Edward of Westminster, meant that Henry unexpectedly found himself as a potential Lancastrian claimant to the throne. The claim, which put Henry at risk from the restored Edward IV, rested upon his mother's descent from Edward III through her father John Beaufort, Duke of Somerset. Although the Beauforts had been excluded from the succession in 1407 by their half-brother Henry IV, Margaret perceived the threat as serious enough to send Henry abroad for his safety alongside his uncle Jasper Tudor in 1471.

Pembroke Castle has been associated with Henry Tudor since his birth. The bronze statue of Henry was erected on Northgate Street Bridge in 2017. (Author's collection)

The castle of Suscinio near Vannes, Brittany. This was one of the castles provided for Henry and his small Lancastrian court in exile by Francis, Duke of Brittany. Largely neglected until 1965, it has since been heavily restored. (Author's collection)

Margaret Beaufort's tomb by Pietro Torrigiano in Westminster Abbey. Margaret was an active participant in her son's rise to the throne and exercised significant authority after his coronation. (Author's collection)

Landing in Brittany, Henry was sheltered by its ruler Francis, Duke of Brittany, who used the Lancastrian fugitives as bargaining pieces to further his domestic ambitions. Various attempts were made by Edward IV and Louis XI of France to secure Henry's custody, and it was not until 1476 that Henry lived more freely at Francis' court. In 1482, his mother came close to securing his honourable return to England, following her third marriage to Thomas Stanley, steward of Edward IV's household. However, Edward's death in 1483, Richard III's subsequent usurpation, and the presumed deaths of the Princes in the Tower opened greater opportunities for Henry's return.

As rumours of Richard III's murder of his nephews spread, so too did plots begin to emerge against the new king. Henry was heavily involved with his mother and Bishop John Morton in the failed rebellion of Henry Stafford, Duke of Buckingham, which broke out in October 1483. Henry was proclaimed king at Bodmin on 3 November, but his departure to England was delayed and he and his fleet arrived to find the coasts of Dorset and Devon occupied by Richard's soldiers. Returning to France without attempting a landing, Henry was joined by some 400 disillusioned Yorkists who had escaped England following the rebellion's failure. At Christmas 1483, Henry vowed to marry Elizabeth of York and received their support and homage in return.

A fresh invasion planned for 1484 was aborted. Soon afterwards, Henry narrowly avoided capture by Pierre Landais, Duke Francis' treasurer, whom Richard III had bribed with offers of English soldiers for Brittany's ongoing war with France. Escaping to the French court, Henry's cause was bolstered when he was joined by John de Vere, Earl of Oxford, a veteran soldier and commander. Together, they secured enough support from Charles VIII of France in money, ships and men to launch another invasion.

The Bosworth campaign of 1485 began when Henry landed at Mill Bay near Milford Haven on 7 August. Proceeding quickly, Henry's small army marched north through Wales, receiving support from the Welsh soldier and landowner Rhys ap Thomas. Entering

England, the army reached Merevale Abbey on the evening of 21 August. The following day, the Battle of Bosworth was fought. Henry's forces secured victory thanks to the efforts of Oxford's vanguard, the French mercenary troops under Philibert de Chandée and the treachery of William Stanley, who threw in his lot for Henry at the last. Richard III was killed on the field, 'struck by many mortal wounds, as a bold and most valiant prince' (*Croyland Chronicle*).

Before the battle, Edward Hall credits Richard with the scathing remarks that Henry was a 'Welsh milksop, a man of small courage and of less experience of martial acts and feats of war … and never saw an army, nor was exercised in martial affairs'. Although the speech is probably Hall's invention rather than Richard's own words, it has helped to create an image of Henry as an unwarlike king without any knowledge of military affairs.

Henry received a knightly education, probably from Sir Hugh Johnys, who had fought for John, Emperor of Constantinople, for five years against the Ottomans in Greece and Turkey. In 1469, aged 12, Henry received a bow and arrows from Sir Reginald Bray, and the same year accompanied his guardian Lord Herbert to the Battle of Edgcote. In 1471, he accompanied Jasper Tudor on a commission to array forces in Wales, and following the Lancastrian defeat at Tewkesbury, they were briefly besieged within Pembroke Castle. These experiences arguably provided Henry with as good a military education as could be expected given his tumultuous early years. As king, he was to show a love for the traditional pursuits of hunting and hawking and was a patron of court jousting. His personal bravery and steely nerve were amply demonstrated during his time in Brittany and at Bosworth. In later years, while not eager for war or personal displays of valour, Henry showed himself perfectly capable of waging war when required and could delegate and choose his commanders wisely.

For Henry's appearance, there are several surviving portraits, although most were painted after his death. Polydore Vergil, who met the king in person in 1506, described Henry as 'slender but well-built and strong; his height above the average. His appearance was remarkably attractive and his face was cheerful, especially when speaking; his eyes were small and blue, his teeth few, poor and blackish'. At their meeting, Henry's hair was 'thin and white', which accords with the words of the Spanish ambassador, Pedro de Ayala, who recorded in 1498 that Henry 'looks old for his years but young for the sorrowful life he has led'. At the time of the Battle of Stoke, however, Henry was 30 years old and in good health. The problems of his later reign, including the accusations of avarice levelled against him, were still many years away.

Henry's principal supporter and battlefield commander was **John de Vere, Earl of Oxford**. The execution of his father and elder brother for treason in 1462 by Edward IV confirmed him as a lifelong adherent of the Lancastrian cause. Although he officiated as great chamberlain of England at Elizabeth Woodville's coronation in May 1465, he was imprisoned in the

Sir Reginald Bray from the north window of Jesus Chapel in the priory church of Great Malvern, Worcestershire. He served as Margaret Beaufort's steward in from 1465 to 1486 and thereafter was one of Henry VII's most trusted administrators. (Author's collection)

The lost tomb of John de Vere, Earl of Oxford, and his first wife, Margaret Neville, that once stood at Colne Priory in Essex. The drawing by Daniel King dates to 1653, when the tomb still survived. (From the British Library: MS 27348)

Tower in 1468 for plotting with supporters of Henry VI. In 1469, Oxford joined Richard Neville, Earl of Warwick (the 'Kingmaker'), and the Duke of Clarence in rebellion against Edward IV and was one of the leading lords of the Readeption regime of Henry VI, being created constable of England. He commanded the Lancastrian right wing at Barnet, but after the Yorkist victory, he turned to piracy and, in 1473, seized St Michael's Mount in Cornwall, where he was besieged. After surrendering, Oxford was imprisoned at Hammes Castle near Calais, but although attainted in 1475 he avoided execution. His imprisonment was not without incident; in 1478, he managed to scale the walls and leap into the moat, probably in an attempt to escape, although some suspected suicide. Richard III ordered his transfer to England in October 1484, but Oxford managed to escape and make his way to Henry Tudor. Returning to Hammes with an armed retinue, Oxford relieved the garrison besieged there and recruited its men into the Tudor army. At Bosworth, Oxford commanded Henry's vanguard and led the attack, fighting directly opposite his cousin, John Howard, Duke of Norfolk, who was killed. It is noteworthy that Norfolk had previously taken care of Oxford's wife during his imprisonment in France. After Bosworth, Oxford returned the favour and made provisions for Norfolk's widow. In return for his aid, Henry VII showered rewards on Oxford, making him the 'foremost man of the kingdom'. He was created lord admiral of England, chief steward of the duchy of Lancaster south of the Trent, constable of the Tower of London, made a privy councillor and initiated into the Order of the Garter. His ascendency ensured his military and political leadership across East Anglia, and he commanded a sizeable retinue. In 1487, Oxford remained one of Henry's principal supporters and his most experienced battlefield leader.

**Jasper Tudor, Duke of Bedford**, was Henry VII's uncle and one of the die-hard Lancastrians throughout the period of Yorkist rule. Knighted and granted the earldom of Pembroke by Henry VI, his half-brother, Jasper was present with the king at the first battle of St Albans in May 1455. He replaced the Duke of York as constable of the castles of Aberystwyth, Carmarthen and

The seal of Jasper Tudor as Earl of Pembroke, c.1459. The obverse shows Jasper in armour, sword raised, on a caparisoned horse. The reverse shows an angel with wings expanded, holding a shield of arms supported by two wolves. (Author's collection)

Carreg Cennen in April 1457 and was created a Knight of the Garter by April 1459. In February 1461, he was defeated by York's son, Edward, Earl of March (later Edward IV), at Mortimer's Cross, after which his father Owen Tudor was captured and executed. For the next 25 years, Jasper was a fugitive, spending time in Brittany and at the French court, occasionally launching attacks against the Yorkist government. In June 1468, Jasper led a small force provided by Louis IX of France to north Wales, taking the castles of Harlech and Denbigh and holding courts in Henry VI's name. In 1470, he was part of the Readeption of Henry VI and travelled to Wales to take control of the principality. Learning about the Yorkist victories at Barnet and Tewkesbury, he was forced to flee with his nephew Henry abroad. During their time on the Continent, Jasper mentored his nephew and shared in his exploits, including the failed invasion of 1483. In 1485, Jasper sailed with Henry on the Bosworth campaign, although no source says he was present at the battle and may instead have remained in Wales to secure Henry's retreat. On the accession of Henry VII, he was rewarded by his nephew with the dukedom of Bedford, restored to the earldom of Pembroke, made lieutenant of Ireland, granted the lordships of Glamorgan, Abergavenny and Sudeley (Gloucestershire), and married Katherine Stafford, widow of the executed Duke of Buckingham, who brought him further lands. Continuing his support for his nephew, Jasper played a significant role in suppressing the rebellions of 1486 and 1487.

Many other leading nobles joined Henry's army for the Stoke campaign. In terms of rank, the most senior were **George Talbot, Earl of Shrewsbury** (also Earl of Waterford) and **Edward Courtenay, Earl of Devon**. Shrewsbury was only 16 or 17 years old in 1485 but participated at Henry's coronation, carrying the sword curtana, and was present at the king's wedding to Elizabeth of York. In 1486, he served on various commissions of the peace. Given his age, his presence at Bosworth is uncertain. At Stoke, he was supported by his experienced uncle, Gilbert Talbot, who had commanded the right wing at Bosworth and probably retained a supervisory role at the head of Shrewsbury's retinue. Devon joined the 1483 rebellion against Richard III but escaped to Brittany. He was knighted by Henry Tudor upon landing at Milford Haven and fought at Bosworth. He carried one of the ceremonial swords at the coronation, sat in council occasionally and attended major court functions. Two other senior commanders at Stoke who had fought at Bosworth were **Sir Edward Woodville, Lord Scales**, and **Sir John Savage**. Woodville was the brother of Queen Elizabeth, the wife of Edward IV. In 1483, he escaped England and probable execution by Richard III with two warships and £10,201 – some 15 per cent of annual royal revenues – in gold coin. This helped to finance the Bosworth campaign, at which Woodville fought as 'a most valiant knight' (*Croyland Chronicle*). In 1486, he went on a crusade to Granada in southern Spain and distinguished himself at the siege of Loja. In the fighting, he lost his front teeth but gained the admiration of Spanish monarchs Ferdinand and Isabella and a reward of 12 horses and two beds. Savage was a Cheshire knight who had fought for Edward IV at Tewkesbury and had become a royal carver, knight of the body, and was one of the chief mourners at Edward's funeral. He was a close family member and associate of the Stanley family and seems to have been mistrusted by Richard III.

An engraving of the tomb of George Talbot, Earl of Shrewsbury, in the Shrewsbury Chapel at Sheffield Cathedral by James Basire, *c.*1750–1800. Talbot had a long and distinguished career in Tudor service and died in 1538. (Author's collection)

The tomb of Sir John Savage in St Michael and All Angels Church, Macclesfield. The *Ballad of Bosworth Field* describes his valour and his men's distinctive white livery hood: 'Sir John Savage, that hardy Knight, deathes dentes he delt that day, with many a white hood in fight, that sad men were at assay.' (Author's collection)

Polydore Vergil says he was 'wholly given to Henry's affairs', advising him to invade and 'take the straight way into Wales'. He commanded the left wing at Bosworth and was rewarded with extensive grants of office and some forfeited estates of John, Lord Zouche, and Francis, Viscount Lovell. Another important commander in the Stoke campaign was **George Stanley, Lord Strange**, eldest son of Thomas Stanley, step-father of Henry VII. He was held hostage by Richard III at Bosworth as a guarantee of his father's loyalty and the king allegedly ordered his execution for Stanley's treachery, although the order was not followed. His father was rewarded with the earldom of Derby and other significant grants after Bosworth. George received the constableship of Pontefract, Knaresborough and Wicklow castles, and was made a chief steward of the duchy of Lancaster. In May 1487, he was created a Knight of the Garter and privy councillor.

## REBEL ARMY

**John de la Pole, Earl of Lincoln**, was the eldest son of John de la Pole, Duke of Suffolk, and Elizabeth, sister of Edward IV and Richard III. Through his grandmother, Alice Chaucer, he had family connections to the Beauforts, and in their youth, his father and Margaret Beaufort had been solemnly betrothed. Suffolk's eventual marriage to a daughter of Richard, Duke of York, was intended as a political reconciliation between previous enemies, but it had the unforeseen result of making their children potential claimants to the throne. John was granted the earldom of Lincoln in 1467 and was often in close attendance at court events. He was knighted and inducted into the Order of the Bath alongside Edward IV's sons in 1475, attended Anne Mowbray at her wedding to the Duke of York in 1478, bore the salt at the baptism of Edward IV's daughter Bridget in 1480, and was chief mourner at the king's funeral in 1483. His opinion of the usurpation of Richard III is unknown, but the de la Pole family provided Richard with unequivocal support at his coronation; Suffolk carried the sceptre and was followed by Lincoln with the orb.

It is probable that Lincoln was with Richard on his northern progress in 1483 and received grants 'for his good service' during Buckingham's rebellion. This included the reversions of several estates on the death of Thomas Stanley that had previously belonged to his wife Margaret Beaufort, valued at £334 25s 5d per year. At the death of Richard's son, Edward of Middleham, in April 1484, Lincoln was appointed chief governor of Ireland and president of the council in the north. Although Richard never formally named an heir, these appointments made it clear that Lincoln was regarded as Richard's probable successor in preference to the Earl of Warwick. Lincoln was in the north during the winter of 1484/85, involving himself in the region's governance, corresponding with the mayor of York and ordering improvements to Sandal Castle.

Lincoln was with Richard at Nottingham on 1 August 1485 and probably fought at Bosworth. He is mentioned swearing to support the king in the *Ballad of Bosworth Field* and the first proclamation of Henry VII's reign incorrectly listed him among the dead. Lincoln escaped attainder and imprisonment – perhaps the 'great and sovereign kindness' to which Henry VII referred after the earl's subsequent defection in 1487 – and appears to have been treated with some favour. He was present at Henry's coronation and was outwardly loyal in 1486 during Lovell and Stafford's rebellion. He led the inquiry into Stafford's treason, was present at the christening of Prince Arthur in September and remained at court for most of the winter until his flight to the Continent. Once he decided to rebel, Lincoln's rank and position as a leading Yorkist claimant made him one of the most serious threats Henry VII would face during his reign.

**Francis Lovell, Viscount Lovell**, was one of Richard III's principal confidants and administrators. During his childhood, Francis' wardship was granted to Richard Neville, Earl of Warwick, through which his friendship with Richard probably began. After Warwick's death at Barnet,

The effigies of John de la Pole, Duke of Suffolk, and Elizabeth of York in St Andrew's Church in Wingfield, Suffolk. John was not implicated in the events of 1487 and was allowed to save the family lands held by Lincoln after his attainder. (Author's collection)

The seal of John de la Pole, Earl of Lincoln. The inscription around the edge of the seal proclaims him as 'nephew of Richard III', probably to publicize Lincoln's position as Richard's heir designate. (Author's collection)

A painting of Francis Lovell wearing armour based on memorial brasses of the 1480s. (© Graham Turner www.studio88.co.uk)

his wardship was awarded to the Duke of Suffolk, who must have introduced him to his son the Earl of Lincoln. Their shared affinity is suggested by Suffolk, Lincoln and Lovell's joint involvement in the Fraternity of the Holy Cross, Abingdon. The proximity of their important Oxfordshire manors, Minster Lovell and Greys Court (owned by Lovell) and Ewelme (by de la Pole), raises the possibility of further social interaction. In 1480, Lovell served under the Duke of Gloucester (later Richard III) in Scotland and was knighted by him at Berwick. In 1483, he was elevated to the rank of viscount, and during Richard's protectorship, Lovell was made chief butler of England. After Richard took the throne, he was promoted to king's chamberlain. His closeness to the king gave rise to the famous couplet by William Collingbourne:

The Catte, the Ratte and Lovell our Dog
Ruleth all England under the Hog.

In 1485, Lovell was sent to guard the south coast against invasion, but he had probably rejoined Richard by the time of Bosworth. Like Lincoln, he was mistakenly counted among the dead, but instead managed to escape and enter sanctuary at Colchester. His actions in 1486 and 1487 show him to be one of the main conspirators against Henry VII.

**Thomas FitzGerald of Laccagh** was the brother and political affiliate of Gerald FitzGerald, Earl of Kildare, the greatest magnate in Ireland. The Kildares asserted themselves during the reign of Edward IV and exploited Richard III's relative weakness to promote Thomas to the role of chancellor. A significant lord in his own right, Thomas built a new castle at Laccagh and obtained several manors from Edward IV in return for service against the Gaelic Irish. Little is known about Thomas' appearance or personality but he may have shared familial traits with his elder brother, who was known for his exceptional charisma and gained admiration as a 'mightie man of stature, full of honour and courage' and a 'warrior incomparable'.

Although not a member of the nobility, arguably the most experienced military leader at Stoke was the mercenary captain, **Martin Schwartz**. Born in Augsburg, a Swiss chronicle claims that he began life as a shoemaker before starting his military career. He served at the siege of Neuss (1475) during the Burgundian Wars and later commanded a force of 200–500 Swiss during the wars of the Low Countries, where he served under Maximilian of Austria. Schwartz gained a reputation for bravery and pitilessness and was a prodigious drinker addicted to rich jewellery. For these traits and others, he was satirized by Maximilian's jester. In the *Herald's Report*, he is described as a 'manly man of war' and

Martin Schwartz shown on horseback surrounded by his men in an illustration from Cassell's *History of England*. In reality, most of the combatants at Stoke fought on foot. (Author's collection)

compared by Bernard André to the Greek hero and warrior, Diomedes, king of Argos. Despite his military experience, he likely underestimated the dangers of the Stoke campaign. He gained posthumous literary fame in England as a character in several Tudor plays and poems.

The rebellion was supported by **Sir Thomas Broughton**, owner of Broughton Tower and one of the principal men of Lancashire North of the Sands. Previously a dedicated Ricardian, Henry VII attempted to gain Broughton's loyalty with grants of land and property, but this did not prevent him from protecting Lovell after the latter escaped to the Furness Fells in 1486. Broughton was granted a pardon by the king but remained opposed to the new regime and Vergil says he was one of the leading conspirators throughout the rebellion. **John Scrope, Baron Scrope of Bolton**, and **Thomas Scrope, Baron Scrope of Masham**, played more equivocal roles in the uprising. John was a staunch Yorkist, created a Knight of the Garter in 1463 by Edward IV, and fought at Northampton, Towton, Hexham and Bosworth. He held many offices and commissions and became a close associate of Richard III. Although he attended Henry VII in 1486 at York, it is unlikely that he had any enthusiasm for Tudor rule. Thomas Scrope was John's younger and comparatively impoverished relative. He came of age and was knighted in 1480, but his involvement in the campaign of 1487 was almost certainly influenced by his elder relative. Although neither fought at Stoke, their actions supported the rebellion.

# OPPOSING FORCES

## HENRY VII'S ARMY

Medieval kings depended on their nobility's support to raise men to fight in their armies. Although 38 English peers were summoned to parliament in 1484 by Richard III, only seven were sufficiently committed to his cause to join him at Bosworth. Despite the great redistribution of patronage that he had carried out, Richard could not inspire or compel the nobles, knights and gentry to support him, a factor that ultimately proved fatal.

Henry VII faced a similar problem. Although there were three dukes, one marquess and 15 earls in 1485–87, this abundance of numbers concealed a dearth of loyalty, talent and power. Only two, Derby in the North-West and Northumberland in the North-East, had established regional power structures. Four others had the means to build such structures: Bedford in South Wales; Oxford in East Anglia; Shrewsbury in the West Midlands and Welsh Marches; and Devon in the South-West. However, Devon was not overly endowed with land, Shrewsbury was still young and Bedford and Oxford had only recently re-established themselves in their localities since Henry VII's victory at Bosworth. Many of the other peers were politically inactive, minors or, in the case of Lincoln and Warwick, actively opposed to Henry and his security. Henry did have the advantage that the crown lands he inherited were far larger than almost any monarch before him, including the principality of Wales, the duchies of Cornwall, Lancaster, York, Gloucester, Somerset, and (temporarily) Buckingham, the Earldoms of Warwick, Chester, Richmond and Ulster, as well as other smaller manors forfeited by those he had attainted. These lordships constituted a huge latent reserve of men and revenue, but without the long-standing regional networks and relationships that could unlock these resources, they could not be relied upon to provide large numbers of fighting men.

The traditional avenues for raising an army were through indentures, by which the higher nobility contracted themselves to fight for the king for an agreed length of time, at a specified sum, with a certain number of men, and promised to bring them to a place of assembly by a fixed date. The higher nobility in turn would have contracts with the lesser nobility, gentry and knights, often their friends, kinsmen, tenants and neighbours. Together, these networks of obligation and reward were enough to assemble a standing army. To ensure that they could field enough men at speed, many magnates maintained a near-permanent force, paying annuities to retain (hence 'retainers') their loyalty and service. In the greatest magnate households, such retainers held offices such as steward or chamberlain, thus reinforcing their bond with their lord. A good example of the relationship between king, magnate and his retainers is contained in the letter from the Earl of Oxford to Sir Edmund Bedingfield, dated May 1487, in which he writes: 'your selffe with the jentylmen and other of the contre, to be redy to do the Kyng servyce, whyche I have shewid un to the Kynges Hyghnes, so that hys Grace ys ryght well content and ryght thankfully acceptyth the same.' Bedingfield, for his part, said that he would follow Oxford in preference to any lord other than the king himself.

Despite the problems of the peerage, it is to Henry's credit that many – Bedford, Oxford, Northumberland, Shrewsbury, Devon, Viscount Lisle, the Lords Clifford, Hastings, Strange, Grey of Codnor, Grey of Powis and Grey of Ruthin – took up arms for him during the Stoke campaign. All of these men were probably able to muster sizeable retinues.

Another group that Henry was able to rely upon at Stoke was the men who had shared his exile, both Lancastrians and ex-Yorkists, many of whom had fought for him at Bosworth. There were also those whose support for Henry had gone back even further to Buckingham's rebellion in 1483. Many of these men had been richly rewarded by the king. For example, Sir John Cheney had been a household knight for Edward IV, acting as a squire of the body and master of the horse, and served in France in 1475 with a retinue of seven men-at-arms and 18 archers. He took part in Buckingham's rebellion but was forced to flee, being attainted in 1484. He was knighted on landing at Milford Haven and fought in Henry's bodyguard at Bosworth, being unhorsed by Richard III himself. His rewards included being created a Knight of the Garter, keeper of the New Forest, constable of Southampton and Christchurch, and steward of Cranbourne, Canford and Poole. This type of service and reward continued at Stoke and the number of men who had previously served in 1483 and 1485 who picked up arms once again was remarkably high. This included many old retainers of William Hastings, Baron Hastings, one of Edward IV's close friends and most important courtiers, whom Richard III had executed. For such men, their Yorkist affiliations were more readily transferred to Henry VII through his marriage to Queen Elizabeth than to a Yorkist pretender.

Below the levels of knights, the yeomen and lesser gentry could enter into another type of contract, known as 'livery and maintenance', by which they agreed to wear the lord's livery – a tunic in his colours and bearing his heraldic badge – and fight for him when called. In return, they received his protection and 'good lordship', which could result in help, protection or career advancement.

Another method of raising men was the commission of array – or raising of the local militia. During the Stoke campaign, Henry issued a commission of array while in Bury St Edmunds on 7 April, directed at the Duke of Suffolk

The Italianate terracotta tomb monument of Sir Edmund Bedingfield in St John the Evangelist Church in Oxborough, Norfolk. (Author's collection)

The effigy of Sir John Cheney in Salisbury Cathedral. His career of loyalty to Edward IV and opposition to Richard III was mirrored by many others. He fought at Bosworth and was made a knight banneret at Stoke. (Author's collection)

and the Earl of Oxford, among others. The commission included orders to repair and maintain the beacons on the Suffolk coast to forewarn 'the coming of the king's enemies'. The same day, Oxford was issued an order to bring men arrayed in Norfolk, Suffolk and Essex to the king and to 'engage the rebels and king's enemies if they should fall in with them'. The following day, commissions were sent to Cambridgeshire, Huntingdonshire and probably other counties across central England. Unfortunately, such commissions did not guarantee a high quality of men or equipment. Around 1480, the response of Ewelme (Oxon) and 17 surrounding villages to a commission included 85 men, 17 of whom were archers. However, 38 of these were 'without harness' (body armour), one had armour but could not wear it, and the weapons the raw levies carried were an assortment of bills, staffs and axes.

Another avenue for raising men throughout the Wars of the Roses was through town and city militias. The *York House Book* says that between 100 and 400 men of York were arrayed at various points in the 1487 campaign. Coventry, Leicester and Nottingham also provided men to fight in Henry VII's army. However, these contingents were not always large; Coventry supplied an average of 100 soldiers according to a contemporary document of 1455 and in 1453 Nottingham could field only 30 archers.

## REBEL ARMY

Lincoln and Lovell could not use the conventional recruitment methods available to Henry VII. Instead, they had the support of Margaret of York and the significant financial and military resources of the Habsburg Netherlands. Activity centred in large part on the city of Bergen op Zoom, whose rulers, the Van Glymes, were supporters of Margaret and her step-son-in-law Maximilian of Austria. Money was raised and equipment supplied, including the delivery of 60 *pavois* (shields) ordered by Margaret from the receiver of artillery. The Lille receipt mentions '400 long pikes … to be distributed among the German-Swiss pikemen, who were then to take and lead across the sea by ship, under the command of my lord Martin de Zwarte'. In early May, a document records the arrival of certain captains and riders before the city gates and the expenses for their ships and provisions. Although they were finally sent elsewhere, their original destination was recorded as 'Ingelant' (England).

A view of the palace of Margaret of York in Malines by Jan-Baptist De Noter, c.1820. The palace was bought by Margaret in 1477 and it was probably here that much of the Stoke campaign was planned. (Stadsarchief Mechelen – Verzameling Schoeffer)

The assembled soldiers were mostly professional German and Swiss mercenaries known as *Landsknechte*. This term, translating as 'servants of the land', was applied to some Low Country infantry units as early as 1470. Their architect was Maximilian of Austria, King of the Romans (from 1486) and later Holy Roman Emperor, who intended to form a professional army in service to the Habsburg dynasty. The background to their foundation was Maximilian's difficult situation in the Netherlands during the 1470s, when cavalry-centred units of knights and men-at-arms had become increasingly vulnerable to pike-wielding professional infantry. He also had the problem that many of his vassals preferred to pay him money or hire mercenaries to avoid armed service in person. Finding the existing mercenary units to be below his expectations and preferring not to hire the Swiss *Reisläufer*, Maximilian recruited men from the Habsburg lands of Austria, the Rhineland and the Low Countries and formed them into fighting bands.

Swiss men-at-arms from Zurich depicted in the *Amtliche Berner Chronik*, c.1478–83. The men carry pikes, halberds, crossbows and arquebus handguns. (Bern Burgerbibliothek, Mss.h.h.I.2, f.141)

The first units were assembled in Bruges in the 1480s and were trained in Swiss pike tactics. As early as the Battle of Sempach in 1386, the Swiss formation of pikemen had proved successful against Austrian knights and men-at-arms. This development continued in the 15th century, notably during the Burgundian Wars between Charles the Bold and the Swiss Confederacy. This training ensured that the *Landsknecht* mercenaries were a formidable fighting force: disciplined, well-armed and confident in their abilities. Each man was required to supply his own weapons and armour, consisting of a doublet, metal helmet, breastplate and sword, and a pike, halberd, firearm or crossbow. However, at Stoke, it is evident that some mercenaries were equipped with armour and weapons supplied by Margaret of York. On another occasion in 1483, Maximilian ordered 600 sallets, 400 armguards, and 1,000 body harnesses to ensure his men were adequately equipped. In 1486, he made an order for 950 ash pikes.

When in battle formations, the *Landskneche* integrated their arms effectively. Their pikes were 15ft to 18ft long, equipped with a 7in. metal tip, and used for offensive and defensive manoeuvres in closed ranks. Armour-piercing 6ft halberds were used for hacking and thrusting, to disarm enemies and unhorse cavalry. Crossbows were phased out of the imperial arsenal in 1507, but were previously used frequently alongside the arquebus. Although Stoke took place before the full flowering of the *Landsknechte* in the 16th century, fighting men fitting this general description made up the body of mercenaries supplied for the 1487 campaign by Margaret of York. Maximilian had recently proved their military effectiveness at Guinegate (1479), at which he dismounted and fought on foot with his men to secure victory over the French. The presence of the nobility alongside them and the favour shown to the *Landsknechte* by their employers caused them to develop a powerful *esprit de corps*. In 1485, Maximilian put his mercenaries at the head of a procession entering Ghent and in 1486, when Maximilian entered Brussels, the military achievements of Martin Schwartz earned him the privilege of being the only man in the procession to enter the city on horseback, including the king himself.

The Battle of Vögelinsegg (1403) depicted in the *Spiezer Chronik* by Diebold Schilling, c.1484–85. The men are shown using late 15th-century armour and weapons. (Bern Burgerbibliothek, Mss.h.h.I.16, f.526)

Another significant component of the rebel army was provided by the Irish. Relative to England, medieval Ireland was a lawless country, marked by constant feuding and warfare. An area of particular friction was the borderland between the 'Pale', the permanent enclave of the English in the counties around Dublin, and the regions ruled over by the native Gaelic. The elite warriors of Ireland between the 14th and 16th centuries were the galloglass (*gallóglach*), the name translating to 'foreign warrior'. They began as mixed Scots, Gaelic and Scandinavians from the Western Isles, driven out of the country by the king of Scots, but soon became naturalized in Ireland. The galloglass were professional, paid soldiers, some retained permanently as household guardsmen for a single lord. Such men were not mercenaries in the true sense of the word and many eventually became subject clans of the

Irish galloglass and kern by Albrecht Dürer, c.1521. The kern wear woollen mantles and have long fringes in a style known as the 'glib', supposedly to conceal the identity of the wearer. The galloglass on the left wears a *cotún*, a form of fabric armour quilted into vertical rolls. The other galloglass carries a bow, an assortment of darts, and an obscenely oversized sword. (Staatliche Museen zu Berlin, Kupferstichkabinett/Jörg P)

greater Irish lords. Other 'freelance' galloglass might spend their entire lives serving in different retinues and looking for military employment. The standard length of service for such men was typically set at a quarter of a year.

Anthony St Leger, a lord deputy of Ireland under Henry VIII, described the galloglass in detail, saying that every one of them had a heavy, long-handled battleaxe or halberd-axe, 'called a spar' (or *tuagh*), which resembled 'the axe of the Tower', by which he probably meant the executioner's two-handed axe in the Tower of London. Despite St Leger's claim about the ubiquity of the spar, galloglass soldiers are frequently depicted wielding spears, one-handed axes, swords (one- and two-handed) and daggers. St Leger described their armour and combat to Henry VIII in 1543 as 'footmen … harnessed in mail and basinets'. In 1428, John Swayne, Archbishop of Armagh, noted the activities of 'eight battles of footmen arrayed in the guise of this country, that is, every man [in an] aketon, haubergeon, pisane, basinet'. As these excerpts suggest, the armour of most galloglass was considered out of date compared to the equipment worn by wealthy Englishmen. Unlike military fashion elsewhere, Irish military taste remained relatively consistent well into the 16th century. In many cases, the galloglass still wore coats of mail, worn over a padded quilt coat (called a *cotún*), which rarely seems to have been paired with any substantial plate armour. Instead, the most substantial body defence was the jack or coat of iron plates, described by Edmund Spenser, a long-time English resident in Ireland and author of the *Faerie Queen*, as 'Of great defence to ward the deadly fear'.

However, trade between Ireland, England and the rest of Europe did exist, and wealthier galloglass would have been better arrayed than others. Some Irish, particularly the nobility, would have been harder to distinguish from English men-at-arms. An example of this trade is found during the reign of Richard II (1377–99) when the English intercepted a ship with 'armour, artillery and other goods and chattels' intended to 'aid and comfort' the king's 'Irish enemies'. Archaeological evidence of galloglass armour and weapons shows they could be extremely well made and highly decorated, inlaid with precious metals.

According to St Leger, the galloglass were always accompanied by 'boys', and John Dymmok, an Englishman who served in Ireland in the late 16th century, said each galloglass had 'a man for his harness bearer and a boy to carry his provisions'. This group of three was known as a 'spar', after the weapon, and a nominal 100 or 120 spars made up a 'battle'. St Leger says that the attendants carried three javelins and in combat would skirmish, retreating behind the galloglass once these were spent, after which the galloglass would advance. If the galloglass were on the receiving end of an attack, their attendants would again skirmish with the approaching enemy, hurling their javelins until, as St Leger put it, 'they come to the hand tripe'.

In 1537, the English judge Robert Cowley wrote contemptuously that 'amongst 200 of them there shall be scant eight gentleman … all the residue [are] slaves … gathered out of divers countries'. He also claimed that they would often keep mailcoats spare, which could be used to equip raw recruits, allowing the leaders to pass them off as experienced warriors and pocket the resulting higher fee. Despite this condemnation, many other sources commend the conspicuous bravery of the galloglass. St Leger says they were 'the sort of men … that do not lightly abandon the field, but bide the brunt to the death'. Nor can it be said that they were always inferior to the English men-at-arms. In 1423, they defeated an English force at Meath and in 1480 an English document called *A description of the power of Irishmen* praised them as being trained for war and 'practised in toils thereof'.

The tomb of Rowland FitzEustace, Baron Portlester, Chancellor of Ireland, who died in 1496. Portlester was the father-in-law of the Earl of Kildare and supported the coronation of 'King Edward' in 1487. His tomb effigy shows him wearing plate armour, but of a type out of fashion in England. (Author's collection)

Another elite Irish soldier was the mail-clad horseman, but considering the journey to England by sea, it is unlikely that many made the crossing, and the sources mention none. It seems probable that most of the Irish sent to England were neither horsemen nor galloglass, but kerns (*ceithearn* or *ceithearnach*), who were poorly armed footmen unable to afford the horse and mail of a horseman. In 16th-century England, the kerns had an evil reputation, well demonstrated by Shakespeare's lines:

My Lord of York, try what your fortune is.
The uncivil kerns of Ireland are in arms
(*Henry VI, part II*)

Shakespeare also describes them memorably as 'shag-hair'd crafty kern' capable of many 'villanies', and has York exclaim that he had seen a man fight against a troop of kern 'so long, till that his thighs with darts were almost like a sharp-quill'd porpentine'. To the English soldier Barnaby Rich, the kerns were 'the very dross and scum of the Country … the very Hags of Hell, fit for nothing but for the gallows'. English hostility was partly bred from aversion to the fiercely Gaelic characteristics of the kern – they were known to be pugnacious fighters, who learned their craft through cattle raids, incessant blood feuds and ambushes.

Dymmok says kerns were 'a kind of footman, slightly armed with a sword, a target [round shield] of wood, or a bow and sheaf of arrows with barbed heads, or else three darts, which they cast with a wonderful facility and nearness, a weapon more noisome to the enemy, especially horsemen, than it is deadly'. Similar to the galloglass, the armour and weapons of the kern remained largely unchanged for centuries, consisting of a sword (*cloidhem*), long dagger (*scian*), bow (*boga*) and set of javelins (*ga*). As early as the 12th century, Gerald of Wales speaks of the Irish going into battle without armour, carrying short spears, axes and darts. Jean Froissart, writing about the Hundred Years War (1337–1453), describes the simplicity of their armour. Although variety no doubt existed between individuals, body protection appears to have been restricted to a helmet, gauntlets and light body armour of a loose tunic (*léine*), often dyed yellow, and coat (or mantle) made from sheep's wool, which could double up as bedding. Edmund Spenser accused the mantles of providing appropriate shelter 'for a thief or rebel'. Nevertheless, he could admire the stoic resilience of the kern, hailing them as 'great endurers of cold, labour, hunger, and all hardness' and 'very great scorners of death'.

# NUMBERS

The earliest estimate of the number of men who fought at Stoke is in the *York House Book*, written in late June or July 1487, based upon the testimony of an eyewitness. It records a total of 10,000 men in the royal vanguard, 20,000 in the rebel army and 5,000 total dead after the battle. It also records that Northumberland and Clifford's combined force numbered 6,000 men on their departure from York, 400 of whom were brought by Clifford, and 4,000 on their return. In the parliament of November 1487, the rebel army was recorded as being 8,000 in number, of whom 28 were attainted. Another contemporary source is the *Herald's Report*, written c.1488–90, which records that 4,000 were slain, although no estimate is provided for the total number of men in either army.

A similar figure of 4,000–5,000 dead is given by Jean Molinet, writing c.1490. However, several of his other estimates are ridiculous. He says that Henry VII had 20,000 men, Lord Strange had 14,000–15,000, and that the royal vanguard was 15,000 strong. Lord Scales is said to have commanded a force of 6,000 men and John Welles, Lord Welles, another 10,000, only to be prevented from reaching the battle due to rumours of Henry's defeat, which caused him to retreat to London. Together, these estimates total an absurd 50,000 men in the royal army. Molinet does, however, corroborate the figure of 8,000 rebels given in the 1487 parliament, of which he says only 200 escaped the field. He also states that the German mercenaries were 1,500–1,600 in number, a more reasonable figure at odds with his other estimates. In Polydore Vergil's account, the number of Germans is slightly higher at 2,000, which number is followed by all other accounts that used him as their source. The author of *The Book of Howth* estimated that '4,000 and more' of his Irish countrymen were killed, but the independent value of this figure is lessened due to its account of the battle being wholly copied from other sources. The only other source to indicate the size of the royal army is Francis Bacon, who says that Shrewsbury, Strange and other knights added 6,000 to the royal army, 'besides the forces that were with the king before'.

Although there is therefore some agreement in the sources about the numbers of the rebels, there is little reliable information about the size of the royal force, besides a general agreement that, as Hall says, 'the kynges army was wonderfully encreased, & from tyme to tyme greatly augmented' until it significantly outnumbered the rebels. Interestingly, the *Herald's Report* says that Lord Strange 'brought with him a great host enough to have beaten the king's enemies, only of my lord his father's … folks and his'.

Luckily, a more accurate idea of the number of men brought to Stoke can be ascertained from the household records of individual lords. The Earl of Oxford's wide patronage meant that he could count on at least ten members of the gentry to give him military service. An indication of the number of men they would each bring is provided by John Paston, who in 1489 wrote to ask whether he could reduce the number of men he brought to the muster from the 20 he had promised. His brother William, serving in Oxford's household, replied that 12 would probably be enough, but that Sir Edmund Bedingfield, Sir Thomas Tyrell and Sir Richard Fitzlewis were all bringing 30 and that to remain high in the earl's favour he 'wolde not ye schulde be to ferre undyr them'. On top of these, Oxford perhaps could count on another 30 men to provide ten men each. Together this meant that around 700 men could be raised from his close followers. On top of this would be the fighting men from his household and tenants, the size of which can be estimated by the stock of his armoury at Earls Colne, which in 1513 amounted to 175 sallets, 101 brigandines, 124 halberds, 140 bills, 120 bows, 64 arrow sheaves, 83 pairs of gussets and 25 *aporns* of mail, perhaps enough for 275 men. On top of these, Walden, Ipswich and Bury sent contingents totalling 204 men in 1487, while other individuals, towns and hundreds in Essex contributed almost £400. Altogether, it therefore might be estimated that Oxford's contingent at Stoke was somewhere between 1,000 and 1,200 men. However, this would have been by far one of the single largest contingents on the battlefield, and the list of known combatants shows that the East Anglian gentry were well-represented compared to other regions.

An English bill and a Swiss halberd from the late 15th to early 16th century. These were among the most common weapons at Stoke Field. Not shown to scale. (Philadelphia Museum of Art, bequest of Carl Otto Kretzschmar von Kienbusch, 1977 [1977-167-451]; Metropolitan Museum New York, gift of William H. Riggs, 1913 [14.25.74])

It is highly likely that only the king, the Stanleys and perhaps Bedford would have been able to muster a similarly large number of troops. Perhaps half this number may be more plausible for lords like Devon and Shrewsbury, especially considering the short time given for the muster. Recent historians have commonly estimated the number of troops at Stoke to be 15,000 for the royal army, of which 6,000 served under Oxford, pitted against 8,000 in the rebel army. However, if Oxford's contingent of no more than 1,200 was by far the largest within the vanguard, there is some reason to suppose these estimates are considerably inflated.

# OPPOSING PLANS

## MOTIVATIONS

When Lincoln arrived in the Low Countries, his high rank and status as the nephew of Richard III and Margaret of York ensured he became the undisputed leader of the rebellion. Vergil says that once he arrived, he met with Lovell and several others, and together they decided to hasten to Ireland to bolster Simnel's credibility as a viable rival to Henry VII. They would then launch an invasion of England with Irish help and, if successful, would 'free from prison their genuine nephew Edward, Earl of Warwick, and then, by the authority of their leading friends, crown him king'.

It is sometimes supposed that the leading rebels were motivated by loyalty to the House of York. Vergil says Lincoln 'could not bring his mind to witness calmly Henry, a man of the opposing faction, on the throne'. However, upon closer examination, it becomes clear that many other personal and local factors influenced their decision. While Lincoln may have intended to place Warwick on the throne and wield power in the king's name, his true and more selfish motivation was almost certainly the throne itself. The positions of office granted to him by Richard III in 1484 are good evidence of the king's favour and reveal a possible intention to name Lincoln as his heir. Furthermore, Warwick's claim had been explicitly disregarded by Richard during his usurpation thanks to the attainder passed on George, Duke of Clarence, by Edward IV, which barred Warwick from inheriting his father's titles, estates and claims. Considering the attainder was never reversed, Lincoln could still make a solid claim to be the rightful Yorkist heir. Defeating Henry VII in battle would have allowed Lincoln to dictate subsequent events, including the crowning of Warwick if he had so chosen. However, his choice to rebel risked everything – his lands, chattels and even his life – without any guarantee of success. While personal animosity towards Henry and the opportunity to wield power behind the throne may have been strong reasons to rebel, Lincoln undoubtedly had loftier ambitions in mind.

The rebel's host and supporter in the Low Countries was Margaret of York. From the beginning, she had refused to accept that Bosworth was the end of the dynastic conflict between York and Lancaster. Henry Tudor's accession also cost her valuable commercial privileges in England, and ended any hope that the remaining portion of her dowry of 200,000 *écus* would be paid. Henry's backing by the French during the Bosworth campaign also opened up the dangerous possibility of an Anglo-French alliance, which

# The rebellion of 1487 and the road to Stoke Field

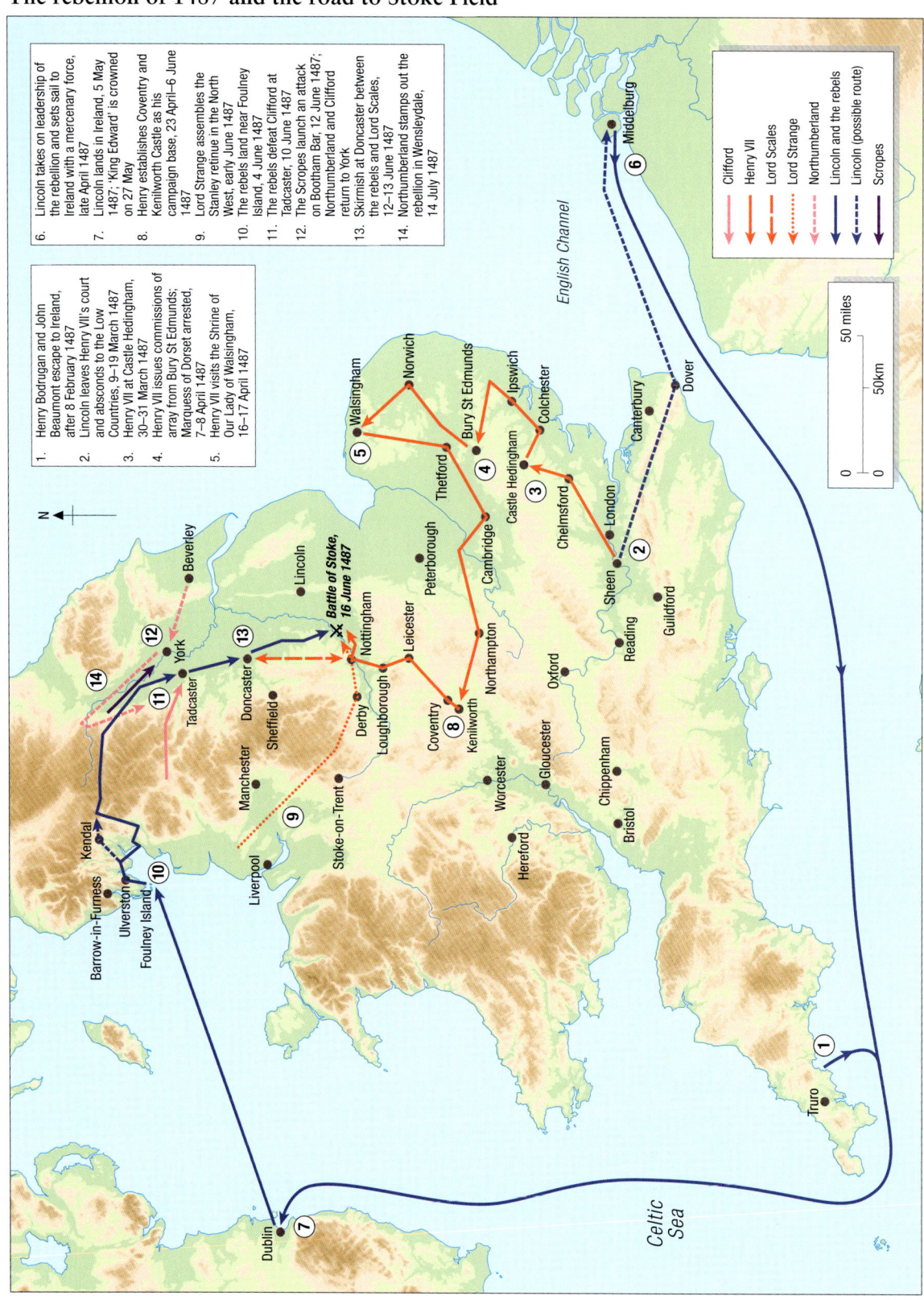

threatened Burgundian interests and security. For that reason, Margaret's efforts against Henry eventually gained the tacit approval of Maximilian, King of the Romans, who had married Mary, Duchess of Burgundy (1457–82), and retained an interest in the Netherlands through their son, Philip the Fair. Margaret's early involvement in the Lambert Simnel plot is suggested by the mention of the gift of wine for the 'son of Clarence' at her court at Malines (modern Mechelen) as early as July 1486, which may also corroborate Molinet's account that the boy briefly visited her court.

The sources suggest that Margaret's personal animosity toward Henry VII was just as significant as any diplomatic concern she felt on behalf of her country. This is perhaps more demonstrative of the sources' prejudice against Margaret as a woman and enemy of the Tudor government than it is an accurate record of her motivations. However, her subsequent backing of additional conspiracies, such as Perkin Warbeck's rebellion in 1497, offers some validation for the assertion.

Other major supporters of the rebellion were the Irish lords and bishops. As far back as 1447, Richard, Duke of York, had been appointed lieutenant of Ireland and was resident there for much of the 1450s. York was the political and dynastic heir of the Lacy and de Burgh families, both of which had played prominent roles in Anglo-Irish history. Therefore, he was viewed as at least partly Irish by the native lords, many of whom eagerly gave him their support. During his time in Ireland, York supported the faction that sought greater autonomy from the English crown and appointed Thomas FitzGerald, Earl of Kildare (1421–77), as his deputy. Thanks to this appointment, Kildare, and later his son and heir Gerald FitzGerald (1456–1513), became the de facto rulers of Ireland. The Yorkist kings, Edward IV and Richard III, were largely forced to accept this situation. Although the crown still appointed lieutenants, including Lincoln in 1484, they governed *in absentia* while effective leadership was exercised by the Kildares, whose dominance even encompassed much of Gaelic Ireland.

Henry VII's accession threatened Kildare's position, as he had previously supported the Yorkist faction and received his last commission from Richard III. Two months after Bosworth, Kildare continued to hold the Irish parliament and issue coins in Richard's name. This led to mutual distrust between Kildare and Henry, although the latter was also forced to acknowledge Kildare's dominance. In March 1486, Kildare's official role as deputy was renewed, nominally under the new lieutenant Jasper Tudor. Kildare was also summoned to the English court, although there is no evidence that he made the journey. Despite their mistrust, Kildare actively negotiated with Henry, and, in 1485, he married his second daughter to the male heir of the Lancastrian Thomas Butler, Earl of Ormond. Meanwhile, general relations between the Irish and English deteriorated, culminating in the Irish parliament authorizing the citizens of Dublin to retaliate against English merchants trading in Ireland in response to previous attacks and robberies against them in England.

This was the situation in Ireland in the run-up to the rebellion. Although Kildare showed some signs of accepting the new government, he was not a natural ally to Henry VII. A continuation of the dynastic conflict in England that had characterized the preceding 30 years could help only to keep royal attention away from Ireland, thereby allowing Kildare to continue his exercise of power. In 1487, Kildare was therefore open to supporting the rebellion

Cotehele in Devon was built by the Edgcumbe family in multiple phases between c.1450 and 1530. The enmity between Sir Richard Edgcumbe and Sir Henry Bodrugan was one of many family rivalries during the Wars of the Roses. (Author's collection)

as a means to maintain and extend his power at home. His actions and by extension those of his brother Thomas, were all calculated towards this end.

Others joined the rebellion out of less lofty ambitions. Sir Henry Bodrugan was a significant landowner in the south-west, at one time called the 'scheff reulere of Cornwayle'. He was regularly commissioned between 1454 and 1486 as a justice of the peace and commissioner of array, and was even occasionally given special tasks such as investigating and dealing with piracy. In 1473, he was briefly in charge of the force besieging John de Vere, Earl of Oxford, at St Michael's Mount. He was later made a knight of the body of Richard III, and was possibly present at Bosworth. Bodrugan was repeatedly accused in chancery, privy council and parliament of a range of violent, extortionary and piratical offences, the most famous being his persecution of Sir Richard Edgcumbe in 1484, who, according to family history, evaded Bodrugan's men by hiding next to the River Tamar near his family home of Cotehele, Devon. Filling his cap with stones and throwing it into the river, Edgcumbe fooled his pursuers into thinking he had drowned, which allowed him to travel to Henry Tudor in Brittany. After Henry's accession, Bodrugan served on one commission, but on 8 February 1487, an order was given for his arrest. At this point, Edgcumbe took revenge by pursuing Bodrugan so vehemently that he only narrowly escaped by leaping over a cliff to a waiting boat. Whether these romantic do-and-dare stories are fact or fiction, Bodrugan was joined by his bastard son, John Beaumont of Tregonan, in Ireland and both subsequently joined the rebellion.

Another rebel was Richard Harlestone, a yeoman of the king's chamber for Edward IV, who helped lead the capture of Mont-Orgeuil Castle in 1468, thereby liberating Jersey from the French. Harlestone was afterwards made captain of the islands of Jersey, Guernsey, Sark and Alderney and is reported by the late 16th-century *Chroniques de Jersey* as a popular governor, encouraging the locals to practise using the longbow. Nevertheless, after Bosworth, he is said to have resisted Henry VII's rule. He attempted to make himself lord of the islands, under the French and Margaret of York's protection, but was thwarted by local resistance. The rumour of Warwick's presence on Guernsey in 1486 hints at Harlestone's involvement in the rebellion that year, and although he was pardoned by Henry, rebellion probably offered him his last chance of returning to his previous eminence on the islands.

Other men who chose to rebel were those who had lost everything from Richard III's downfall and Henry's accession. The most senior was Francis

Lovell, whose personal antagonism towards Henry as Richard's close friend must have been mixed with resentment over his lost estates and status. Many others further down the social scale had been similarly disadvantaged. Robert Percy's father and namesake had fought and died for Richard III at Bosworth. In 1483, the elder Robert had been made comptroller of the household, and possibly also captain of the king's guard and a privy councillor. In February 1484, he and his wife were granted seven manors in Norfolk and Essex, formerly belonging to Elizabeth, Countess of Oxford, and in March 1483, he received three further de Vere properties in Cambridgeshire, plus reversion of further manors on the death of Thomas, Lord Stanley. Together these lands expanded his income considerably compared to his relatively meagre patrimonial lands around the village of Scotton, near Knaresborough in Yorkshire. After Bosworth, Robert was not posthumously attainted, but Oxford and his wife recovered all the lands he had gained. The younger Robert was therefore left to deal with the loss of his father and any chance of the promising career and lifestyle that had seemed assured during the brief years of Richard's reign.

A similar story also accounts for the three or four members of the Harrington family who joined the rebellion. After the death of both the senior male figure and heir of the family at the battle of Wakefield, the surviving Harringtons had been plunged into a bitter dispute with the Stanley family over the legal descent of their lands, including the family seat of Hornby Castle. Edward IV imposed a compromise, but the Harringtons' loyal service to Richard while he was Duke of Gloucester reignited their hopes for a full restitution upon his accession. However, their participation at Bosworth resulted in two of the family, James and Robert Harrington, being attainted and the former may even have been killed. The Stanleys, meanwhile, were rewarded by Henry VII for their decisive role in the battle, giving the Harringtons little hope of recovering their patrimony except through rebellion.

While the motivations for rebels were varied, for Henry VII and the men who benefited from his government, their motivation was simple – to maintain the position they had gained after Bosworth. For Henry, defeat could mean only humiliation and death, both for himself and his son, Prince Arthur. A similar fate would no doubt await Oxford, Bedford and many of Henry's other principal supporters. Among the lesser men of the Tudor regime who might hope for clemency if the rebellion proved successful, many still had reason to fear the loss of the offices, lands and incomes they had gained. Such men flocked to join Henry's banner, motivated by self-interest as much as any affiliation they may have felt for Henry VII and his new government.

# THE DUBLIN KING

> So rude a matter and so strange a thinge,
> As a boy in Dublin to be made a kinge.
> (The mayor of Waterford's letter' in Croker's *Popular Songs of Ireland* [London, 1839])

In late April 1487, the English rebels and the mercenaries under Martin Schwartz departed the small harbour town of Arnemuiden in the

Lambert Simnel carried through Dublin on the shoulders of Great Darcy.

'King Edward' carried through the streets of Dublin on the shoulders of William Darcy of Platten, known as 'Great Darcy' on account of his exceptional height. Although depicted as an unkempt giant dressed in Irish garb, Darcy was in fact a gentleman known to 'werithe gowne and dublet' in the English manner. (Author's collection)

municipality of Middelburg and set sail for Ireland. Their movements must have been closely watched by Henry's agents and it may be that he had explored ways to hinder or harry their journey. On 15 April, Henry had authorized regular payments for a new 700-ton ship being built in Kent, overseen by Sir Richard Guildford, and later in the same month Thomas Rogers, clerk of the king's ships, was paid 26s 8d for his expenses in going to Harwich and victualling the king's ships there. The other purpose of the fleet was to protect the English coast and prevent the rebels from landing. The sea journey probably lasted around 12 days. Although the *Chronicle of Zeeland* (1551) gives the departure date as 15 May, this must surely be incorrect as a letter from Henry VII to the Earl of Ormond sent on 13 May says that the rebels had already landed in Ireland on the 5th of the same month. Arriving in Dublin, Lincoln and the others were probably welcomed by the other English rebels, including Sir Henry Bodrugan.

By this point, Simnel had already been in Ireland for some time. When he arrived in Dublin, probably in late 1486, Simnel was given a warm greeting by Thomas FitzGerald and lodged by him, probably either at Thomascourt just outside the city walls or in his new castle at Laccagh. Vergil says that FitzGerald immediately believed the boy to be Warwick and called together his inner circle to convince them 'both for his own sake and that of the boy' that he was the sole surviving heir of York and 'that each man ought to strive to restore him to his ancestral kingdom'. FitzGerald would have known of Warwick's partial Irish lineage through his grandfather the Duke of York, and that his father the Duke of Clarence had been born in Dublin Castle. Warwick could therefore be claimed to some degree as an Irish prince. A large council was soon called, probably at Dublin Castle, at which the other peers, lords and bishops were persuaded or coerced into his support, almost certainly with the approval of Kildare. This group probably included Edward Plunket, chief justice of the common pleas, and James Ketyng, the Hospitaller prior of Kilmainham, who were both later 'noted to be the chief causes of the great rebellion late in Ireland'. The council agreed to send messages to the chief towns of Ireland, Margaret of York and Richard III's old supporters in England to inform them of the arrival of the Yorkist youth and ask for support on his behalf. However, one mystery in these events is the existence of a pardon 'for all manner of treasons' given to Thomas by his brother Kildare, dated 8 December 1486. It is unclear what treasons are referred to or why such a pardon was necessary. There is a possibility that this was for Thomas' role in harbouring Simnel, and may be connected with Henry VII's actions and 'secret business' in Ireland. However, Thomas retained his chancellorship and Kildare's subsequent support for the rebellion makes it highly unlikely that Kildare was unaware or disapproved of Thomas' actions. There is also no proof that the assembled Irish were anything but genuine in their belief that the boy, imposter or otherwise, was truly who he claimed to be.

When Lincoln arrived in Dublin events proceeded quickly, no doubt spurred on by the presence of the large number of mercenaries quartered around the city and the need to keep up momentum. The coronation of 'King Edward' was rapidly organized and took place, either on 24 (according to Henry VII's parliament of November 1487) or, more likely, Sunday 27 May 1487, a more appropriate ceremonial day attested by several Irish sources. A suitably sized crown for the boy-king was sourced from a statue of the Blessed Virgin Mary, which then stood in St Mary's Church, Dam's Gate. During the ceremony in Christ Church Cathedral, the Bishop of Meath gave a sermon reciting the boy's claim to the throne. In a letter to Henry VII written after the events, Octavian, the Italian-born Archbishop of Armagh, claimed that he had raised objections to the 'profane crime of crowning a child in Ireland'. This caused Lincoln to fly into a rage and approach the Earl of Kildare seeking 'power and license to execute the royal rights', but he was calmed and dissuaded from violence. This is noteworthy, as it suggests that Kildare was the person in control of events in Dublin, despite the presence of Lincoln and his mercenary army. Moving on from this improper display, the coronation proceeded, and Walter Fitzsimon, Archbishop of Dublin, placed the borrowed crown on the boy-king's head. After the ceremony, a joyous procession to the castle passed through the streets, with the new king in its midst, carried on the shoulders of Sir William Darcy of Platten and Janico Markys, the Mayor of Dublin. Although he absented himself in fear for his life and possessions, the Bishop of Armagh then reports that the Earl of Kildare held a 'great council of the aforesaid crowned by a certain name', at which the lords spiritual were also present. Interestingly, Armagh does not specify the exact regnal name. Still, surviving letters patent issued by Kildare, and two handwritten records of a lost writ in the name of 'Edward VI' to the Sheriff of Uriel, destroyed in 1922, provide some evidence that the Irish believed it was Edward, Earl of Warwick, who had been crowned rather than Prince Edward, son of Edward IV, who would have taken the regnal name of Edward V. Coins were probably soon struck at the Dublin mint, with an inscription of 'REX HIBERNIE' – 'king' rather than the traditional title 'lord of Ireland'.

The view of Christ Church Cathedral by Robert Pool and John Cash, *c.*1779, before its Victorian renovation. (Author's collection)

Coin with the arms of England and three crowns, traditionally associated with Lambert Simnel. Some variants of this coin include the inscription 'REX ANGLIE FRANCIE ET REX HYBERNIE'. (Redrawn from the original in the Fitzwilliam Collection, author's collection)

Arms of Gerald, Earl of Kildare, formerly in St Mary's Chapel, Christ Church, Dublin. Family legend caused the ape to be adopted as the family's heraldic supporter. 'Crom a Boo' was the traditional FitzGerald war cry. (Author's collection)

There were those in Ireland who shared the Bishop of Armagh's feelings. Thomas Butler, who was later made keeper of the Irish chancery rolls, informed Henry VII of the 'great and abominable treasons and insurrections' that had taken place in Ireland and was subsequently jointly attainted by Kildare with his brother William Butler. The *Book of Howth* says that Nicholas St Lawrence, 'perceiving all this but a mad dance', also sent word to Henry, although if this is true his later pardon for involvement in the affair is difficult to understand. The city of Waterford notably abstained from the widespread acclamations of the boy-king's coronation and remained loyal to Henry. The mayor, John Butler, responded to a letter from Kildare charging him to receive and support the new king by sending men to fight for his cause with the desultory answer that the boy crowned in Dublin, 'whosoever he may be', had no right to the throne and that those who supported him were 'rude enemies, traitors, and rebels, to the right prince and king of England'. A poem written by Butler and others in 1488, addressed to the Archbishop of Dublin, further ridiculed the coronation and argued that it had been 'a plain digression unto their true liegance unto rebellion' and laid stress upon Queen Elizabeth's rights and claim as heir to Edward IV.

Other than the coronation, the weeks in Dublin gave time for the assembly of the Irish host. It was decided that this should be led by Thomas FitzGerald, who resigned his role as chancellor to join the rebellion. He was assisted by Maurice fitz Thomas, a 'Geraldine' relation, as well as Edward Plunket the younger, probably the son of Edward Plunket of Balrath, a former seneschal of Meath and a younger son of the first lord of Killeen. The contingent must have included many of Kildare's Gaelic Irish allies, the O'Neill, O'Reilly and O'Connor Faly clans, all of whom would later fight for Kildare at Knockdoe (1504). With their preparations made, the rebels set sail with their mercenary and Irish allies on 3 June.

# 'KEPING OF THER TRUTHES AND DUE OBBEYSAUNCE UNTO US'

When Henry heard of the early events in Ireland, he acted swiftly, first by investigating the claims and then by displaying the 'real' Warwick to dissuade further treachery. Pardons were offered to all those who would return to their allegiance. His difficulty was that it was unclear who was behind the rebellion and how far it extended. When Lincoln absconded to the Low Countries, Henry can have been in no doubt that a serious conspiracy was forming against him. However, with enemies in Burgundy and Ireland, the king could not have been certain where the attack would come from or to what extent the two sources of rebellion were connected.

Until 28 March, Henry remained in the London area, then began a royal progress through East Anglia. His intention must have been to show himself to the people, ensure their loyalty and prepare for a possible invasion from that direction. Suffolk was the focus of de la Pole power, concentrated around the castle at Wingfield. East Anglia was also where the Duke of Norfolk, killed fighting against Henry at Bosworth, had mustered his men. Henry therefore was accompanied by a large retinue of Lancashire and Cheshire gentry, retained in September 1486 for the prodigious sum of almost £1,000. The progress allowed him to discuss the forthcoming campaign with Oxford, whose military acumen was completely trusted. Henry stayed at Oxford's residence at Castle Hedingham on 30–31 March, where he may also have spent some more pleasurable time engaging in court dalliance following Oxford's previous 'grete boste of the fayre and goode gentylwomen of the contre'. The progress then continued to Colchester, Ipswich and Bury St Edmunds, where the Marquess of Dorset was arrested and the first

Castle Hedingham was the seat of the de Vere family. Much of the castle was rebuilt by Oxford in the years after Stoke, but today only the 12th-century keep survives. (Author's collection)

commissions of array were sent out. Lincoln's father, the Duke of Suffolk, headed the list of those to organize the array, and joined the king, the earls of Oxford and Derby, Lord Fitzwalter, Steward of the Household, and Sir Robert Willoughby, to celebrate Easter at Norwich. The king then travelled to Walsingham to pray and give an offering at the Shrine of Our Lady.

Contented that he had done what he could in East Anglia and assured of Suffolk's loyalty or probable inaction, Henry turned and travelled at great speed to Coventry, which he reached on 22 April. It is possible that some news of trouble precipitated this sudden action, for it caused Henry to miss the Garter celebrations on St George's Day, which he had celebrated the year before with great solemnity.

In its central location in the west midlands, Coventry was an excellent place for Henry to await events and muster his army. It also had the benefit of being a traditional Lancastrian stronghold and was conveniently close to Kenilworth Castle, where Henry himself took up residence between 8 May and 6 June. Back in East Anglia, however, the wide-ranging powers to raise troops given to Oxford had an unexpected reaction when Lord Fitzwalter summoned several important gentry members to Attleborough and told them that Oxford's commission was illegal and that as the Steward of the Household, he had precedence. His instructions that they should not march with Oxford caused some confusion. Sir William Boleyn of Blickling and Sir Henry Heydon of Baconsthorpe returned home and Sir Edmund Bedingfield sent letters to Oxford, receiving a reply that the rebels had gone to Ireland and the king would not put Bedingfield to any 'further labour or charge'. However, Oxford cautioned Bedingfield to be ready to serve 'upon reasonable warning'. Oxford's letter also included the interesting detail that Henry was considering sending an army to Ireland, probably one of the many ideas Henry was contemplating to counter the rebellion.

This uncertain situation caused widespread alarm, as demonstrated by the correspondence between the king and the city of York. On 22 April, Henry wrote to bid them keep watch for the rebels. The next day they sent a letter asking for help rebuilding the city's defences and arming the castle. The king was able to send money 'in caas that the Kynges ennvmes approche thiddre' but said that he 'hath yit noo certain knowlage when his ennymes woll take ther shipping'. Meanwhile, they could take the artillery they needed from Scarborough Castle where 'twelve serpentynes, some more, some less, of diverse sortes garnysshed with chambre and powder' could be found. On 1 May, Henry thanked the city for 'observyng and keping of ther truthes and due obbeysaunce unto us' and on 4 May, he was able to send word that the rebels had departed westwards from Flanders and that the city 'shal not nede to have any strength or company of men of werre for this season'. However, this did not stop seditious words from being uttered in York Minster that the city's people would not tolerate alien knights and men-at-arms being brought within the walls. Such whispers suggest growing anxiety about the rebellion and how it could affect the city. To compound these issues, William Welles, a former mayor, was murdered while commanding the watch at Bootham Bar. While reacting to this shocking event, the city authorities were informed by the constable of Scarborough Castle that he could not send his guns, because he had only four and they were all required for the castle's defences.

Rumours also spread like wildfire. On 3 June, Henry issued a proclamation ordering that anybody caught uttering 'feigned, contrived and forged tidings' should be set in the pillory for as long as the authorities deemed suitable. Some took the chance to spread untruths against individuals for political and personal reasons. On 29 April, John Paston received a letter from Thomas Balkley saying that Lord Fitzwalter falsely suspected him of departing the country by ship and had 'imagined and purposed many grievous things' against him. Ominously, there were other matters Balkley did not feel safe to commit to paper but promised to tell Paston at their next meeting. In another letter, it was said that Paston had talked with Lady Lovell, wife of the rebel Francis, at Barkway in Hertfordshire. These malicious rumours, however, came to nothing when Sir John Paston proved his loyalty by fighting for Henry VII at Stoke.

At Kenilworth, news of Lincoln's arrival in Ireland had reached Henry by 13 May. At this point, if not before, Lincoln's intention to invade England in support of the impostor must have become clear. Henry responded by sending for the queen and his mother, knowing that it would probably be the last chance to spend time with his family before the invasion. He also asked the Queen's Chamberlain, the Irish peer Thomas Butler, Earl of Ormond, to meet with him to discuss Irish affairs, probably to better understand the Irish force he was likely to face. Jasper Tudor and the Earl of Derby were still with him to offer advice, though several of the other lords had returned home to raise their retinues. At Coventry, the army was already beginning to form and Sir Reginald Bray negotiated loans from the city of London to ensure the soldier's pay and supply of victuals.

The Great Hall and inner apartments of Kenilworth Castle, added by John of Gaunt, Duke of Lancaster, in the late 14th century. Henry stayed here with his family awaiting the invasion. (Author's collection)

Kenilworth must have been frenetic with activity as the king and his government prepared for the invasion. Henry's surviving correspondence shows he received messages from across the kingdom, sending orders in response. Intelligence must also have been received daily, with spies informing the king of the rebels' actions and his suspected enemies in England. On 22 May, two men believed to possess information about the rebellion were sent from York for questioning. Soon after, news of the coronation in Ireland must have arrived, much to Henry's displeasure.

The king's preparations can be seen through several of his letters and proclamations. On 4 May, he wrote to the Archbishop of York asking that the papal bull threatening excommunication on any who disputed his royal title be promulgated at Furness Abbey and Cartmel Priory in

Piel Castle is a 14th-century fortress built by the abbot of Furness to guard Barrow-in-Furness against pirates and Scots raiders. The rebels landed nearby in 1487. (Brian Morris, © The English Heritage Trust)

north-west Lancashire, a strong indication that this area was an expected point of invasion. On 5 June, instructions were sent north that every town and victualler should provide his men with bread, ale and horse-fodder 'at reasonable price in ready money'. The next day, Henry issued a stern proclamation, under pain of death or bodily punishment, to both civilians and soldiers, that there should be no robbing or spoiling of churches or private individuals, no troubling of persons for previous offences unless given the king's express command, that women should not be ravished, that food should not be taken without paying a reasonable price, that nobody should hinder victuals being sent to the king's army, that the king's men should be ready to fight, that nobody in the king's army should raise their voices or blow horns after the watch had been set, that no vagabonds or common women follow the king's army, and that all men should be ready to obey their officers.

At some point in April, Vergil says that Christopher Urswick, the king's clerk and almoner, and a native of Furness, was sent north to report on the depth and defensibility of potential harbours against the rebel fleet. On his way back to court, he was overtaken by a courier bearing news of the rebels landing and urgently 'sent ahead a messenger to tell the king of the approach of his enemies, and following on the heels of the messenger, himself gave a full account of the matter'. Vergil also says that the king had dispatched 'squadrons of cavalry both to keep watch for his adversaries' arrival and to arrest certain men come from Ireland so he might learn his enemies' plans'. Once Henry knew of the invasion, probably on 7 or 8 June, he immediately travelled to join his growing army in Coventry.

## INVASION OF ENGLAND

The rebels landed on June 4, traditionally at Foulney or Piel Island. While the rebel leaders may have briefly visited the island's castle, its small size and isolated location in the Walney Channel must have forced the rest of the army to make land elsewhere on the Furness Peninsula. The landing site was well chosen. There was little hope that the counties of Devon or Cornwall would rise in their favour, Wales would fiercely support Henry VII and the traditional areas of Stanley power around the Ribble and Mersey estuaries were some distance to the south. Furness also offered an easy route to Wensleydale in Yorkshire, a district with deep and historic affiliations with the Houses of York and Neville.

One of the first to greet Lincoln and the newly crowned boy-king was Sir Thomas Broughton, one of the principal conspirators whose fortified residence at Broughton Tower was nearby. His retinue and several other local supporters were quickly added to the army. By tradition, the rebels are said to have camped their first night at Swarthmoor near Ulverston, which may or may not be named after Martin Schwartz. Ironically, this march would have taken them past Gleaston Castle, owned by the same Marquess of Dorset who had recently been imprisoned in the Tower. The other significant landowner in the area was the abbey of St Mary of Furness, but there is no evidence that the monks offered any meaningful support to the rebels. They were probably mindful of their recent promulgation of the papal bull favouring Henry VII and that Christopher Urswick's father happened to be one of their lay brothers.

On 5 June, the rebels began their long march into Yorkshire. Their route would have taken them past Newby Bridge, Kendal and Sedbergh into Wensleydale, passing by Hawes, Castle Bolton and Middleham. It is equally possible that the army took a less direct, though not necessarily more time-consuming, route through Cartmel and over Morecambe Sands before turning north through Lonsdale past Hornby Castle. This would explain the indemnity of 100 marks later paid to the king by the prior of Cartmel and the mention of 'Scantfort', perhaps Carnforth, in Molinet's account. The same author also says that this is where the army was met by several supporters, perhaps the Harringtons and Middletons.

The army was probably well received in Wensleydale due to the area's recent association with Richard III. On 7 June, the army may have rested the night in the environs of Jervaulx Abbey, as the abbot, William Heslyngton, was later forced to seek a pardon. On 8 June, the army continued to Masham, from which a letter was penned and delivered to the mayor of York in the

The impressive arched entrance to the chapter house at Furness Abbey. Although a number of leading men in the Furness area strongly supported the 1487 rebellion, the abbot and monks took no major part. (Mike Kitson, © The English Heritage Trust)

name of King Edward, asking for entry into the city for rest and victuals. However, the city authorities answered curtly that the people of York would not allow them to enter the city and would defend it stoutly 'with their bodies'. Copies of the letter were then sent to the Earl of Northumberland and the king.

As disappointing as York's response must have been, the more pressing concern was the lack of Englishmen joining the rebel cause. Some supporters had met the army on its march and been added to their ranks. At Kendal or Sedbergh, they were probably joined by Clement Skelton of Bowness, Alexander Appleby of Carlisle and Nicholas Musgrave of Brackenthwaite. They also received support from Richard Redman, Abbot of Shap. However, when they entered Yorkshire there was no mass uprising in their favour and the peerage mostly remained aloof. The local esquiers John Pullen of Scotton, Edward Franke of Knighton, Thomas Metcalfe of Nappa and Richard Knaresborough all joined, but while the Barons Scrope of Bolton and Masham probably offered to help the rebellion, neither committed themselves conclusively by adding their retinues to the army. The speed of the rebel advance into Yorkshire may have taken them and others by surprise, but this would assume Lincoln had sent no warning of their arrival. It may be that the failure of Lovell's 1486 rebellion in the same region dissuaded men from joining in 1487 or that the government had already spread propaganda denouncing their figurehead as an impostor. *The Great Chronicle of London* says that Martin Schwartz complained to Lincoln that the earl had deceived himself and Schwartz with his previous confidence of attracting popular support, but remained committed to the campaign to fulfil his promise to Margaret of York.

David Baldwin's study of those attainted in the parliament of November 1487 in connection with the rebellion, and those subsequently pardoned between 4 August 1487 and 11 August 1489, lists almost 100 names. Of these, however, it is impossible to know how many took part in the battle (as opposed to simply offering support) and the number of men each brought with him to fight. In 1475, Baron Scrope of Bolton had served in France with

The ruins of the domestic range at Jervaulx Abbey. Its monks may have given shelter and support to the rebels on their march and the abbot was later forced to seek pardon for his actions. (Author's collection)

Bolton Castle in Wensleydale was the fortress and family home of the Scropes of Bolton. Perched high on the sides of the valley, it would have been visible to the rebel army on their march. (Author's collection)

20 men-at-arms and 200 archers, but he was an important nobleman with significant resources. It may be that Sir Robert Broughton, the Harringtons and some of the other rebels were able to bring a good number of men, but most of the known individuals who fought were not of sufficient status to be capable of mustering large numbers.

Lincoln could not afford to wait long in hope of attracting significant reinforcements. On 9 June, the rebel army crossed the River Ure at Boroughbridge and continued south without troubling York. A rapid advance was crucial to success, just as it had been for Henry VII two years earlier at Bosworth. Lincoln may also have been aware that forces were already mustering against him, both around the king and in the north itself.

On 6 June, just two days after the rebel landing, the Earl of Northumberland wrote to York from his manor at Leconfield (140 miles from Furness), informing its citizens of the invasion and warning them to prepare. On 8 June, he wrote to the city again promising his aid. The other force moving toward York was that of Lord Clifford, who arrived on 9 June at Mickelgate Bar with 400 men and received a gift of wine from the city, 'according to his honour'. At noon the next day, Trinity Sunday, Northumberland arrived with a much larger force. That afternoon, Lord Clifford departed and 'took his journey towards the king's enemies lying upon Bramham More, and lodged himself that night at Tadcaster'. Whether this was part of a stratagem agreed with Northumberland or Clifford was acting on his own initiative is unclear. Considering his numerical inferiority, the plan may have been to harry the rebels as they advanced south. However, his movements were tracked by enemy scouts, and the rebel army attacked Clifford's camp during the night. With their proficiency in raids and skirmishes, it is conceivable that the Irish kerns led the attack. Clifford was able to escape back to York, but many of his retinue, including the armed men of York who had joined him, were 'maimed, slain, despoiled and robbed', according to the *York House Book*. Embarrassingly, Clifford's travelling trunks and packing chests were lost to the rebels.

The main rebel host carried on its march south to Doncaster. Two days later, at 11 o'clock on Tuesday 12 June, Northumberland, Clifford and 'many other nobles' departed the city intending to join the king's army farther south. Some delay was caused by Clifford and the survivors returning to the city on

**THE ASSAULT ON BOOTHAM BAR, YORK, 12 JUNE 1487 (PP.52–53)**

Shortly after Northumberland and Clifford marched out of York, the Scropes arrived at the city and launched an attack on the gates at Bootham Bar. The *York House Book* gives a short account of the action: 'the Lordes Scropes of Bolton and Upsall, constreyned as it was said by there folkes, cam on horsbak to Bowthom Barre, and ther cried King Edward, and made a salt at the yates, bot the Comons being watchmen there well and manly defendid tham and put tham to flitht'. Although their men may have had Yorkist sympathies, it is far more likely the Scropes were themselves the instigators of the attack, planned with Lincoln and the other rebel leaders to distract and separate Henry VII's supporters. Here John Scrope, Baron Scrope of Bolton **(1)**, can be seen conferring with his junior colleagues Thomas Scrope, Baron Scrope of Masham and Upsall **(2)** and Sir Edmund Hastings **(3)**. Their men wear murray and blue liveries prominently featuring the white rose of the House of York **(4)**. In front of them is Bootham Bar, the scene of several violent incidents in 1487, defended by Mayor William Todd and his men **(5)**. York Minster, in which seditious words were spoken in May 1487, can be seen in the background **(6)**. Although the attack on the gates was abortive, it achieved the objective of forcing Northumberland to return to the city without providing further support to Henry VII. The excuse of being coerced by their men later proved expedient when the Scropes had to explain their actions to the king.

Monday morning, but Northumberland may have been content to hedge his bets, as he had at Bosworth, by not seeking to engage the enemy directly. When he had gone some six miles and was approaching Tadcaster, he was overtaken by messengers from the city. At noon, only an hour after Northumberland's departure, the two Barons Scrope had arrived on horseback at Bootham Bar and assaulted the gate. The men of York had resisted them and put them to flight after some difficulty. The mayor had then ridden through the city with 100 armoured men and proclaimed in the name of King Henry that all freemen and residents of the city should immediately arm themselves and attend the wardens at their posts. Any non-resident of the city 'in harness' was immediately to leave the city by the south gate or face imprisonment and loss of his armour. The *York House Book* says that the Scropes were 'constrained by their folks', implying that their tenants had forced them into this action. This seems unlikely as the evidence suggests they were joined willingly by their associate Sir Edmund Hastings, whom ironically Henry VII had sent to the city's aid a few weeks earlier. It cannot be proved whether the Scropes were acting in concert with the rebels or were pursuing more personal interests, but the former option is far more likely and their men are said to have shouted in favour of King Edward. Their assault also had the immediate effect of inhibiting those loyal to the king from marching south. Northumberland decided to turn his men around and sent messengers to ask the mayor to be allowed to re-enter the city 'for diverse considerations and causes him moving'. When they returned, the mayor caused the street of Micklegate 'to be garnished with men in harness', perhaps as a precaution, but in the event Northumberland and Clifford were welcomed back into the city without incident. On 14 June Northumberland then headed north, sending letters over the next few days from Richmond, Fountains Abbey and Leconfield. He must have calculated, correctly as it turned out, that the four-day delay had prevented any possibility of his arrival in time for the battle. His route from Richmond to Fountains Abbey may have taken him through Middleham and Masham, and although it is unrecorded, his purpose may have been to ensure that any discontent in these areas was firmly stamped out.

Bootham Bar and York Minster in 2024. The gate's barbican was demolished in 1835. It is nevertheless a remarkable survivor, together with York's other remaining medieval walled defences. (Author's collection)

## TO STOKE FIELD

The choice about who should command the royal army was decided early in the campaign. Jasper Tudor, Duke of Bedford, was assigned to command the king's battle, which probably included numerous veterans of Bosworth such as Sir Rhys ap Thomas and Sir John Cheney. Oxford 'desired and besought' the conduct of the vanguard (or foreward), the position of greatest honour and danger, which was granted to him just as it had been at Bosworth. Edward Grey, Viscount Lisle, would serve under him, as would a number of the senior lords such as the Earl of Shrewsbury, the Earl of Devon, the Lords Hastings, Ferrers of Chartley and Grey (both Codnor and Ruthin), along with a 'great

The *Medieval House Book of Wolfegg Castle*, written c.1480, is richly illustrated with images of medieval military technology. Folio 51–52 features a military baggage train with rows of wagons surrounded by horsemen and men-at-arms. (Redrawn from the original by the author)

number of other bannerets, bachelors, and esquiers'. The vanguard would have two cavalry wings, the right under Lord Scales, Lord Grey of Powis, Sir Charles Somerset and Sir Richard Haute, and the left under Sir Richard Pole. These men were then immediately sent north as 'foreriders' with other gallants of the king's household as an advance guard to scout the rebel army.

At Coventry, the Bishop of Winchester took his leave of the royal army and returned to Kenilworth to attend the queen, leaving his retinue under the leadership of his nephew, the Earl of Devon. The army then moved to Leicester, passing within a few miles of the battlefield at Bosworth. Arriving in Leicester on 10 June, Henry may have contemplated the similarities between his situation and that of Richard III two years earlier. It was from Leicester that Richard had marched out to confront Henry in battle and afterwards it was in the church of the Greyfriars that his body had been hastily buried. More happily, Leicester had a strong historical affiliation with the House of Lancaster, centred around the castle and the collegiate foundation of Our Lady of the Newarke. While in the city, Henry acted upon his recent proclamations and many 'common women and vagabonds' were imprisoned, 'wherefore there was much more rest in the king's host, and the better rule'.

At Leicester, Henry parted company with his chancellor, Archbishop John Morton, who committed his men to the Earl of Oxford. The next stop was at Loughborough on 11 June, where the king had to deal once again with unwanted camp followers. Many were imprisoned or put in the stocks. The following day, the army kept on their journey north and camped in the fields 'under a wood called Bonley Rice' (Bunny) before approaching Nottingham on 13 June. The next day the *Herald's Report* says that the marshals and harbingers of the army could not find any proper ground for the camp and that 'the king and the army wandered here and there a great space of time'. Luckily, it was a 'royal and a marvellous fair and well-tempered day' and eventually the army came to a 'fair long hill where the King set his folks in array of battle, that is to say, a bow and a bill at his back'. After this, the foreward was 'well and warily lodged under the hill to Nottingham ward' while the king rode three miles to a 'gentleman's place' for the evening. The men in his battle were left to camp in a bean field nearby. Although it is difficult to be certain, the household accounts record a stop at a place called Redhill, north of the city. Nearby is the royal hunting lodge of Bestwood, perhaps the 'gentleman's place' Henry stayed overnight.

That evening, certain spies who had spread rumours that the king had fled were captured and the next morning they were summarily hanged on the ash tree at the end of Nottingham Bridge. The *Great Chronicle of London* reports that many of the king's subjects on their way to join the royal army

# Army movements around Nottingham, 12–16 June 1487

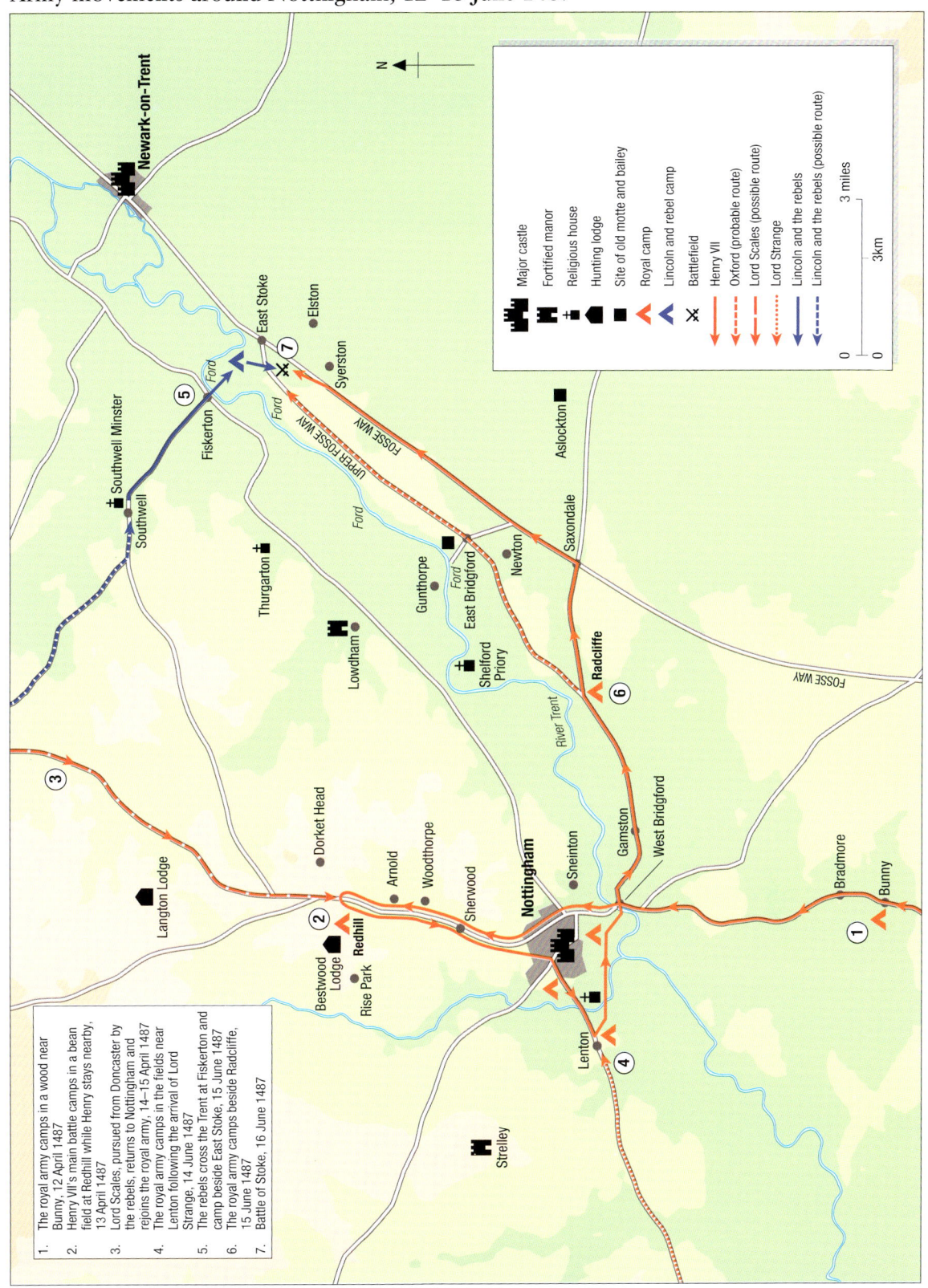

were waylaid by these reports in the belief that the king had already lost the field. Molinet's account that Lord Welles turned 'like the others in flight' appears to confirm that these rumours were widespread and that they had a significant leeching effect on the numbers of men reinforcing Henry's army. In his account, Francis Bacon even suggests that many of these men were all too happy to believe the reports and gain a reasonable excuse not to fight. The most likely instigators of these rumours were Lincoln, Lovell and their supporters such as Abbot Sante of Abingdon. Unfortunately for the rebels, it is unlikely that they were the only side using agents and spies to their advantage and there is no reason to fundamentally disbelieve Edward Hall's comments that Henry 'was in hys [Lincoln's] bosome and knewe every houre what the Earl did'.

Whatever information his scouts did tell Henry, they were not able to help the advance force under Lord Scales when they encountered the rebel army. Molinet says that the two forces met at Doncaster and thereafter the rebel army closely pursued Scales from encampment to encampment so that he 'was driven back for three days on end [and] forced to fall back in great haste through the forest of Nottingham'. Although Molinet does not describe any actual fighting between the two sides, it is possible that some limited action did take place and that Scales was forced to retreat in haste. His original orders may have been to join Northumberland and to attack or harry the enemy as a larger army, but regardless of the plan, the pace and scale of the rebel army caught Henry's supporters unawares. Molinet even says that on news of the rebels' success against Scales, the city of York declared for King Edward, but this is not corroborated by any other source and considering the city's earlier resistance to the rebels it seems highly unlikely.

Back in the vicinity of Nottingham, the king celebrated divine service on the morning of 14 June in a local parish church and then, without telling the army of his intent, rode back the way he had come to welcome George Stanley, Lord Strange, and his men from Lancashire and Cheshire marching towards the city from the north-west. When the rest of the army saw the Stanley retinue arrive 'all fair embaytailled', it caused many to marvel, and this impression was probably reinforced when the king himself reappeared with his standard unfurled later in the day, acclaimed by the Garter King of Arms. Perhaps the purpose of this dramatic entrance was to counteract the rumours of the king's flight and to boost his men's morale through a dramatic demonstration of the king's presence and resoluteness. His effort to welcome Lord Strange also demonstrates the importance Henry placed on Stanley's forces and their incorporation within the main body of his army. Whatever the true significance of these events, the whole scene is reminiscent of a similar episode at Bosworth, before which Henry is said to have disappeared to spend the night at a gentleman's house, only to reappear the next morning with promises of support.

Lenton Priory was a Cluniac monastic house located just over a mile south-west of Nottingham. Its fields were used by the royal army to camp on 14 June. (Author's collection)

The rest of the day was spent in musters and manoeuvres and the army encamped that evening to the

The River Trent at Fiskerton. In 1487, the river was much wider and shallower than today, perhaps no more than 50 yards wide and 2ft deep. (Author's collection)

south-west of the city: the king's battle around Lenton, Strange and his men in the meadows to the west and the vanguard by Nottingham Bridge. By this stage, the rebels' journey south must have become common knowledge and that evening, as well as on the eve of the battle, the *Herald's Report* says there were great 'scries' and panicked shouting throughout the camp. On each occasion, the king and the other leaders were soon up and in good array, but many men either fled or took the opportunity to abscond. The herald, who was present, and could well remember the atmosphere and gossip within the camp calls them cowards and says that he 'heard of no man of worship that fled, but rascals'. One of the reasons for these alarms was probably the arrival of Scales with what remained of the vanguard, whose hasty retreat in the face of the rebel force must have caused the rest of the royal army some concern and despondency.

The *Herald's Report* says that the day before the battle, the king moved his army to the south of the Trent and camped beside the village of Radcliffe, conveniently located near the Fosse Way. Vergil, however, says that Henry advanced to Newark to meet the approaching enemy, 'and having lingered there a little while, he continued for three miles, and there he pitched camp and spent the night'. As an eyewitness, the herald is clearly to be preferred, but it remains possible that Henry sent men ahead to Newark to maintain the loyalty of the town and its castle, and to prevent the rebels from crossing the river over the town's bridge.

After Doncaster, there is no record of the precise route taken by the rebels southwards. However, since Molinet records that they chased Scales for several days through the forest of Nottingham and the *Herald's Report* says they passed by Southwell, it is possible that they took the road from Bawtry to Ollerton or a more westerly route through Worksop and Mansfield. Throughout their march, Vergil says the rebels purposefully did not harm any towns or villages, since they wished to encourage men to join their ranks. However, few men south of the Humber flocked to their cause and George Ascough and his brother were the only two Nottinghamshire men of significance recorded as fighting with the rebels at Stoke. As they approached Nottingham, there were several possible fording points across the Trent. Before his attainder, Lovell had owned the manor of Stoke Bardolph near Nottingham, but this was probably considered too close to the city and Henry VII's waiting army. On 15 June, they marched through Southwell to Fiskerton, where a bend in the river and the wide, shallow waters provided a perfect crossing. As evening drew on, Lincoln and the rebels waded across the river before marching a little under a mile towards the small village of East Stoke and the Church of St Oswald's just visible on the distant horizon.

# THE CAMPAIGN

## THE BATTLEFIELD

The king and his army would have risen before sunrise. Henry heard two masses in the parish church of Radcliffe, led by Richard Fox, Bishop of Exeter. Throughout the camp, men would have been preparing their armour and weapons, and, if there was a priest available, hearing mass and confessing their sins. Henry and his nobility would have taken special care to show themselves, talk to their men and instil a sense of confidence, and the king rewarded some of those who had demonstrated conspicuous allegiance to his cause with knighthood. Men who already held this honour could be promoted to knight banneret, giving them the right to lead soldiers under their heraldic banner (square flag). Sir Gilbert Talbot, Sir John Cheney and Sir William Stonor, who had each served Henry previously with distinction, all received this honour. These chivalric displays were calculated to foster the recipient's loyalty and build a sense of camaraderie, cementing their bond with the king.

Radcliffe lies around 9 miles from East Stoke and the *Herald's Report* says that Henry drew on the local knowledge of 'five good and true men of the village of Radcliffe, which showed his grace the best way for to conduct his host to Newark, which knew well the country, and showed where were marshes, and where was the river of Trent, and where were villages or groves for bushments [ambushes], or straight ways, that the king might conduct his host the better. Of which guides the king gave two to the Earl of Oxford to conduct the foreward, and the remnant retained at his pleasure'.

**BELOW LEFT**
St Oswald's, East Stoke. Although largely rebuilt in 1738, the church still retains its 13th-century tower. In 1487, the leper hospital of St Leonard probably stood nearby. (Author's collection)

**BELOW RIGHT**
The battlefield photographed from the air. The line of the Fosse Way can be seen running through East Stoke village. The Upper Fosse runs diagonally from East Stoke up to the top of Burham Furlong, where much of the fighting took place. (Christina Belton)

The ancient Roman Fosse Way, still the main road to Lincoln, was perhaps only two miles from the camp at Radcliffe. The herald's testimony that the local guides were split between the king and Oxford suggests the two may have taken separate roads to the battlefield. If this was the case, it is possible that Oxford's vanguard followed the more direct route, known as the Upper Fosse Way, which closely follows the course of the Trent. This smaller road went through East Bridgford and Kneeton before it converged back with the main road at East Stoke. This also accords with the description in the *Herald's Report* of marshes and other problematic features less likely to be encountered on the main road. Certainly, if Henry had followed Oxford directly and remained in close contact, it seems doubtful that the king would have needed to retain three guides of his own. Advancing in two lines along separate roads also had other advantages. It would reduce the length of the column that would result from the whole army marching along the same route and shorten the time required for deployment when they reached the field of battle.

John Chapman's 1794 map of Nottinghamshire shows the traditional location of the battlefield and the area of heathland or 'moor' known as Flintham Lings to the south-west. Today, the ridge to the east of the battlefield is entirely covered by trees. (Reproduced with the permission of the National Library of Scotland)

At East Stoke, the rebels would also be readying themselves for the battle. Similar to the royal army, religious observances would have been heard even though only one priest, Richard Simons, is recorded as being present. Lincoln and the other leaders were probably camped near the church and the hospital of St Leonard, a leper house, whose mastership had been in the gift of Francis Lovell before his attainder in 1485. The rest of the army would have encamped in the surrounding fields. After the previous 12 days spent on the march, during which they had covered nearly 200 miles, many of the men must have felt some weariness. The general morale of the rebels, however, was arguably relatively high considering their recent victories against Clifford and Lord Scales. This must have encouraged Lincoln and the other commanders despite their disappointment over their lack of English recruits. Indeed, the *Great Chronicle of London* suggests that Schwartz 'sped them toward the field with as good a courage as he had had twenty thousand men more than he had'.

In common with many other battles of the Wars of the Roses, most of the sources for the battle provide few details concerning the battlefield tactics, action and sequence of events. Only André, Molinet and Vergil give more than cursory accounts, and these all require careful analysis and scrutiny. To present a narrative of the battle it is therefore necessary to interpret these literary sources in combination with an assessment of the historical terrain, limited archaeological evidence, local tradition and by drawing inferences from the military history of the period.

Fortunately, all the sources agree that the battle took place at Stoke, and unlike other battlefields of the period, there has been general agreement about the location of the battle. The *York House Book* gives more information than most when it says the battle took place 'on the more beyond Newark'. This would seem to conform to the geography of the land immediately to the south of East Stoke, which rises to a high point of 187ft (57m) above sea level at Burham Furlong or Burham Hill. To the east of this high land, there is a gentle slope down towards the villages of Elston and Syerston, but to the west, the land falls away sharply, forming a ridge or escarpment along the line of the Trent. A ravine or gully, known as the 'Red Gutter', interrupts the northern end of the ridge, and drops down to terminate near the modern lane running from Fiskerton towards Stoke. This picture is slightly complicated by our limited understanding of the historic terrain and landscape as it existed in 1487. The only documented area of historic heath or 'moor', known as Flintham Lings, is located in Flintham and Syerston townships, 1km to the south of the currently recognized location of the battle. On this basis, Flintham has more recently been proposed as a possible alternative location for the battle. However, it is entirely plausible that the historic extent of the moor was greater in 1487, encompassing the traditionally accepted battlefield site.

In 1487, the village of East Stoke was larger than today and extended from the Fosse Way to St Oswald's Church. Around it and other villages nearby were areas of ancient enclosure and farmed land. Beyond these confines, it has not been established which areas were cultivated through ridge and furrow or left as common land for grazing. John Chapman's 1794 map of Nottinghamshire shows that there has been little significant change to the immediate area south of East Stoke from the late 18th century to the present day except for the growth of woodland on the escarpment between the battlefield and the Trent. Farther to the south, Syerston Airfield, opened during World War II, has sadly obliterated the Upper Fosse and the lanes that ran between it and the Fosse Way.

No source talks about the weather during the battle, suggesting that it had no significant effect. The harvest in 1487 was generally poor, perhaps indicating that the year was hot and dry.

## REBEL FORMATIONS

The system of command for the rebels is unknown. 'King Edward' was merely a figurehead and although present at the battle was probably not consulted or informed about the military plans formed supposedly on his behalf. Although he was the leader of the rebellion, Lincoln had limited military or battlefield experience, much like Lovell and perhaps also Thomas FitzGerald. Sir Thomas Broughton, Sir James and Sir Robert Harrington arguably possessed greater experience, fighting variously at Blore Heath, Ludford Bridge and in the Scottish campaign of 1482, but none was a

Looking up the slight rise to the top of Burham Furlong with the old route of the Upper Fosse running up the hill. The rebels probably began the battle close to the line of trees. (Author's collection)

significant enough man to have previously held high command. Sir Richard Harlestone had led men to military success on Jersey, but of all the leading rebels it was Martin Schwartz who had by far the most experience in combat and commanding large numbers of men. He must also have had a greater awareness of recent developments in warfare, tactics and weaponry on the Continent. What is unclear, however, is how this experience and the command of his mercenaries translated into authority over the other leaders.

Whatever their level of battle experience, the English leaders would have been proficient in the use of arms and were probably familiar to some degree with the military treatises of the day, such as Vegetius' *De Re Militari* and its 15th-century English verse translation, *Knyghthode and Bataile*. The knowledge of those with better educations perhaps extended to foreign works such as Christine de Pizan's *Livre des fais d'armes et de chevalerie*, with its discussions of more contemporary changes in warfare and technological developments such as artillery. What such knowledge could not overcome, however, was the unbalanced composition of the rebel army. Although the German mercenaries were professional, well-armed and equipped soldiers, the rest of the army must have contained far fewer English billmen and longbowmen than was usual for English armies. Furthermore, the Irish galloglass and kerns presented an unknown element, with more experience in raiding, skirmishing and small-scale warfare than pitched battle. Language barriers must also have caused a significant problem throughout the army.

An Austrian sallet attributed to Adrian Treytz the Elder, c.1480. Sallets were one of the two basic types of helmets in use during the 15th century. (Rogers Fund, 1904, Metropolitan Museum of Art, New York)

Given their disparate composition, the problems of communication and the relatively small size of their army, it seems there was little choice for the rebels other than to form into a single group or battle. Molinet certainly says that they fought in a single massed unit rather than dividing into the usual arrangement of two or three separate battles. Unfortunately, the sources do not provide much information about how this single battle was composed. Vergil says the Germans were set in the front line, probably due to their greater experience, reputation and status as paid men. However, it is highly unlikely they were restricted to the front line, as the pikes they carried were most effective when used in dense ranks. Beyond that, we cannot say with any confidence how the men were arranged. It seems unlikely that the rebel formation was divided into three groups based on nationality. This would defeat the object of massing into a single battle and could threaten the entire army if one section decided to flee. Instead, the army was probably organized into smaller segments, perhaps each containing a complement of English, Irish and German men. Alternatively, each small segment may have been entirely composed of a single nationality but interspersed evenly throughout the rebel formation.

The rebels' sea voyage and march through England must have hindered the inclusion of large-scale artillery, but considering their growing ubiquity during the Wars of the Roses, it seems likely that some mobile pieces were transported to the battlefield. These would have been placed at the front lines and primed for action. The bowmen and mercenary crossbowmen would have stood in front of the men-at-arms, or possibly massed at the wings. At many other battles, notably Blore Heath and Northampton, 6ft stakes were driven into the ground in front of the archers for added protection against

An infantry breastplate 'in the German style', made in Northern Italy, c.1480. By this date, Italian plate armour was being mass produced in large workshops and was becoming increasingly common equipment for ordinary foot soldiers. (Worcester Art Museum, Massachusetts, USA, Worcester Art Museum/ The John Woodman Higgins Armory Collection/ Bridgeman Images)

cavalry and frontal attacks. It is possible that the rebel army would also have included a small number of cavalry to protect the flanks. However, most of the horses would have been kept behind the lines for their owners to mount should the enemy break or attempt to escape should the battle go awry.

Even if it was uncertain how these men would work together in battle, the army must still have presented a formidable sight. The standards and banners of Lincoln, Lovell and the other English men-at-arms, set permanently on the fly with buckram, would have soared over the heads of the men. Nearby, the standard of FitzGerald, proudly featuring the family badge of an ape, would have lent an exotic touch to the display, as would the foreign and many-varied banners of the German mercenaries. Above all the others, the arms of England would have been particularly prominent, proclaiming the legitimacy and presence of the boy crowned as King Edward. Old Yorkist and Neville heraldry, raised over so many other battlefields during the Wars of the Roses, reappeared once again. Many of the men would be wearing a variety of colours, badges and insignia. The German mercenaries regularly wore crosses of St Andrew and St George sewn onto their doublets, and their armour, made in the German gothic or Low Countries fashion, could be even more distinctive. Such armour, often kept 'black' (not polished) to lower the cost, allowed the owner to decorate it as they saw fit with bold and elaborate painted designs. The Irish kerns on the other hand stood out just as prominently due to their conspicuous lack of armour, as well as their yellow mantles and characteristic haircuts. Before the army could be seen, they could probably be heard. The sound of the fife and drum played by the Germans was new in England and would have alerted the enemy to their presence from several miles away.

André and Vergil agree that the rebels advanced to the brow of the hill – almost certainly Burham Furlong – and there 'lay in wait' for the royal army to arrive. Although there is reason to doubt the number of 8,000 rebels given in the sources, it does allow us to calculate the approximate area such a number would have occupied on the battlefield. Vegetius estimated that each soldier required a width of 3ft when standing at order, meaning that if the rebel battle had six ranks their front line would have extended around 4,000ft. Assuming the rebels were oriented towards an enemy approaching from the south-west, this would mean that the line of battle stretched from the top of Burham Furlong to a point slightly beyond the Fosse Way at the bottom of the slope. While this is possible, it conflicts with the scant evidence in the available sources regarding the importance of the high ground. It would also make the line extremely lengthy, making communication extremely problematic. This raises the possibility that the rebel line had an alternative orientation along the same axis as Humber Lane, allowing the entire army to face down the hill. This, however, creates the problem that any army approaching along the Upper Fosse would immediately be presented with the rebel flank upon arrival to the battlefield. Either option is possible, and there are many uncertain variables we cannot currently answer. It may be that the rebel army was smaller than recorded or arranged more than six ranks deep, thereby reducing their frontage. Equally possible is that Vegetius' estimation does not accurately account for the reduced area needed for pike formations fighting in denser groups. An important consideration is that the *Herald's Report* strongly suggests that part of the royal army moved along the Upper Fosse. This makes it far more likely that the rebel formation stood at an angle of approximately 90° to the road, but this remains an educated guess which only further battlefield archaeology can hope to establish. Vergil's suggestion that the rebel army faced Newark can be discounted due to his mistaken placement of the royal camp to the north of the town on the eve of the battle.

## OXFORD ARRIVES

All the sources agree that Oxford engaged the rebels without the support of the rest of the army and that the king's battle remained uncommitted or absent. As the *Herald's Report* says, the 'forward reconnoitred his [Henry's] enemies and rebels, where by the help of Almighty God, he had the victory'. No mention is made of the king's battle. Vergil explicitly states that 'the vanguard alone was engaged'. Given the obvious disadvantage to Oxford of not waiting until the whole army was present before battle was joined, it is uncertain whether this was by accident or design.

The tomb of Sir Richard and Eleanor Croft in Croft Church, Herefordshire. Their careers spanned the Wars of the Roses and included service to Edward IV, Edward V, Richard III and Henry VII. Croft was one of the bannerets created at Stoke. (Author's collection)

It was not unusual during the Wars of the Roses for the vanguard to march well ahead of the main body of the army. At Towton, the Yorkist vanguard commanded by Lord Fauconberg operated some distance in front of the rest of the army for much of the campaign. Indeed, the day before Towton, Fauconberg fought independently and secured victory over the Lancastrians at Ferrybridge. At Bosworth, Oxford led the vanguard in an attack while Henry Tudor's smaller battle remained behind.

One of the reasons the vanguard could operate independently is that it tended to contain the best and most mobile soldiers within the army. At Stoke, Oxford's battle included most of the peers, their household men and retinues. Molinet says that the vanguard was joined by two cavalry wings, one led by Lord Scales and the other by Sir John Savage. If we suppose that many of the other men in the vanguard were also mounted, at least for the journey to battle, perhaps contrasting with a greater number of unmounted men in the king's battle, this adequately explains why the vanguard would have taken a different route to the battlefield and why they arrived first. The Italian monk, Dominic Mancini, describes the English practice of travelling to the battle on horseback and then dismounting to fight:

> Not that they are accustomed to fight from horseback, but because they use horses to carry them to the scene of the engagement, so as to arrive fresher and not tired by the fatigue of the journey: therefore they will ride any sort of horse, even pack-horses. On reaching the field of battle the horses are abandoned, they all fight together under the same conditions so that no one should retain any hope of fleeing.

Although we cannot be sure which of the two routes Oxford followed, his earlier arrival makes it more plausible that the vanguard marched to the battlefield along the Upper Fosse. Alternatively, it may have been thought

# The battlefield and deployment of the royal and rebel armies

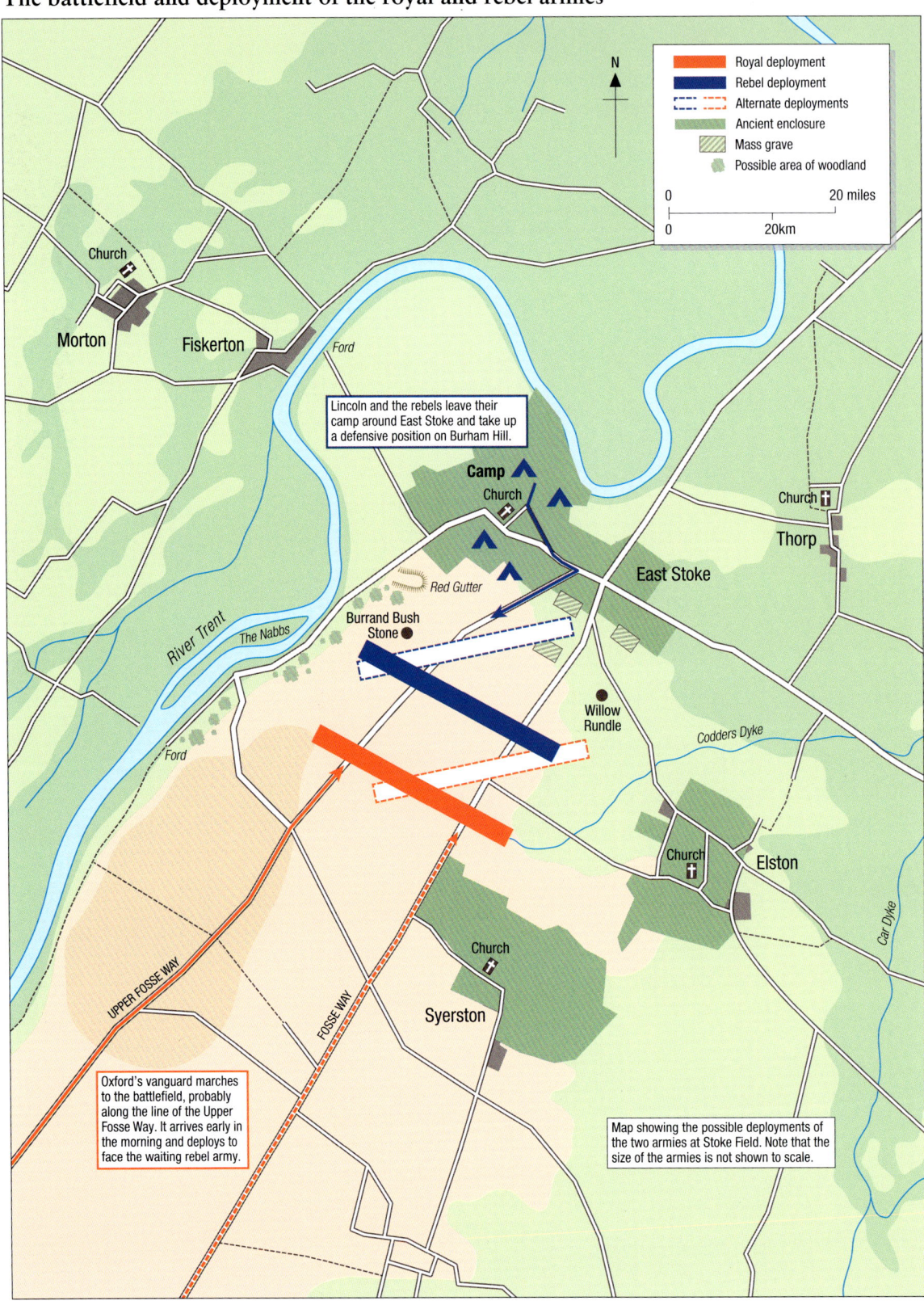

that the mounted men would find it easier to ride along the main route of the Fosse, leaving the rest of the army to take the shorter road. Interestingly, the *Herald's Report* mentions the army were concerned about 'bushments' or ambushes along the road, similar to what happened earlier in the campaign at Tadcaster and Doncaster.

Oxford and the vanguard arrived at the battlefield before 9 o'clock. With the rebels already in position, there would have been a need to deploy quickly and efficiently, and Oxford and the other commanders would have been busy issuing orders and directing their men. The deployment into battle formation would have been conducted in sight of the enemy, but far enough away to dissuade an immediate attack. However, as the men filed into position it must have become clear to both sides that Oxford's battle was outnumbered by the rebels. King Henry's battle and his reserve, commanded by Lord Strange, were presumably some distance behind.

Molinet says that Oxford deployed in the centre of his formation and set his cavalry wings to either side. Lord Scales was set on his right with 2,000 men and Sir John Savage took up the position on Oxford's left with the remaining 1,200. This uneven division fits in with the terrain of the battlefield. The escarpment beyond Oxford's left meant there was little chance of being outflanked from that direction, but the flatter ground on the right of the battlefield posed a greater risk, especially if faced with superior numbers. Once in this basic formation, most of the mounted men would have dismounted to fight on foot in the manner described by Mancini. The archers would then have been sent to the fore to stand in front of the ranks of billmen and men-at-arms, described in the *Herald's Report* as a 'bow with a bill at his back'.

# THE BATTLE

Lincoln and the rebels had probably expected to fight a defensive battle in which they could hold the high ground of Burham Furlong. The arrival of a single enemy contingent presented the unexpected opportunity to attack and defeat it before the rest of Henry's army could arrive. This did not guarantee success as Oxford's vanguard still constituted a dangerous adversary. Lincoln and Lovell in particular would have recognized many of the standards of their fellow peers, and the glint of plate armour clustered around these banners would have made it clear they represented the elite of Henry's army. Nevertheless, a delay would give time only for the rest of the royal army to arrive and reduce the rebels' chances of victory.

Through his military education, Lincoln may have been familiar with Jean de Bueil's *Le Jouvencel*, which warned commanders that 'everywhere and on all occasions that foot-soldiers march against their enemy face-to-face, those who march lose and those who remain standing still holding firm win'. This had been proved correct during many battles of the Wars of the Roses, but on occasion, the maxim could be broken. At Bosworth, Oxford himself had led his men forward across unpromising terrain and defeated Norfolk's larger vanguard. The number of peers in Oxford's battle could also be reckoned as an opportunity. If the rebels could replicate Oxford's success at Bosworth, many of the rebel commanders might be captured or killed in the ensuing rout. This would likely cause such widespread panic among Henry's less seasoned forces that it could easily result in a retreat or general collapse of his army.

**THE MELEE, BATTLE OF STOKE, 16 JUNE 1487 (PP.68–69)**

After the arrowstorm, the rebel army and Oxford's vanguard clashed in fierce hand-to-hand combat. Bernard André states that at one point the ferocity of the rebel attack caused many to believe they had overcome their enemies. For his part, Vergil says that the 'battle was fought boldly and bitterly on both sides. The Germans, fierce mountain men, experienced in war, who were in the front line, yielded little the English in valour; while Martin Schwartz their leader was not inferior to many in his spirit and strength.' Here, John de Vere, Earl of Oxford **(1)**, and his household men fight desperately to weather the onslaught of the rebel attack. Beside him, one of his principal retainers, Edmund Bedingfield of Oxburgh Hall, fights in his support **(2)**. Oxford's standard featuring his device of the blue boar **(3)** flies near him with the banner of George Talbot, Earl of Shrewsbury, a short distance away **(4)**. Facing them, one of the German-Swiss mercenaries fires an arquebus at short range to devastating effect **(5)**. The English knights Sir Thomas Broughton **(6)** and Sir James Harrington **(7)** lead the rebel front line in an attempt to reach Oxford and slay him quickly. In the distance, the standard of Thomas Fitzgerald, the leader of the Irish forces, can be seen advancing towards the royal line **(8)**.

A view of the north side of the battlefield from Burham Furlong towards the steep escarpment. The River Trent and Fiskerton can be seen in the distance. (Author's collection)

Although the rebels had a greater incentive to advance, the sources are not clear on how the battle was joined. André says that the royal army rushed to grab their weapons 'like doves before a black storm' and 'approached the line of the barbarians'. In André's account, however, this enthusiastic action is immediately preceded by a battlefield speech by the king. His soldiers' eagerness for battle can therefore be taken as a literary device designed to show the rousing effect of the king's words.

Vergil says the opposite of André and states that when Lincoln was offered the opportunity to fight on even ground 'the Earl brought out his forces, gave his men the signal, and joined battle'. Vergil's placement of the two sides and his description of the landscape is incorrect, but the basic premise that Lincoln ordered an advance is probably accurate. This meant abandoning the advantageous high ground atop Burham Furlong and any defensive emplacements they had established. Even so, this sacrifice still constituted their best hope of success.

Another possible reason for Lincoln abandoning his position was the 'arrow storm' unleashed before the hand-to-hand combat could begin. In his well-known account, Mancini says that the English and Welsh archers possessed bows and arrows which were 'thicker and longer than those used by other nations, just as their bodies are stronger than other peoples', for they seem to have hands and arms of iron. The range of their bows is no less than that of our arbalests [crossbows]'. Longbows (or warbows) of 100–120lb draw weight were in regular issue during the Wars of the Roses and could launch an arrow approximately 755–1,050ft (230–320m), depending on the skill and strength of the man shooting. Each archer might have as many as 48 arrows at his disposal during a battle, placed in front of him in the ground. In many English armies of the period, archers made up most of the fighting force and, in 1475, the English army taken to France by Edward IV may have favoured archers over men-at-arms by a factor of seven to one. At Stoke, the ratio of archers was probably less extreme and the number in Oxford's battle might have been approximately equal to the number of billmen – perhaps 2,800 each supported by 400 men-at-arms. If an archer could shoot between 6 and 10 arrows per minute, somewhere between 16,800 and 28,000 arrows might land on an enemy army every minute. In the time between the two sides entering a suitable range and closing for the hand-to-hand melee (approximately 3 minutes), a staggering 50,400 to 84,000 arrows might therefore have been loosed from Oxford's side alone, enough to incapacitate and psychologically drain their enemies.

During the storm, arrows were not fired at random but in co-ordinated waves to the command of 'notch', 'draw' and 'loose'. The small amount of

**ROYAL ARMY**
1. Oxford
2. Sir John Savage
3. Lord Scales
4. English longbowmen and mobile artillery
5. Henry VII and Lord Strange

Note: the base map area is 1.9 x 1.5 miles (3 x 2.44km).

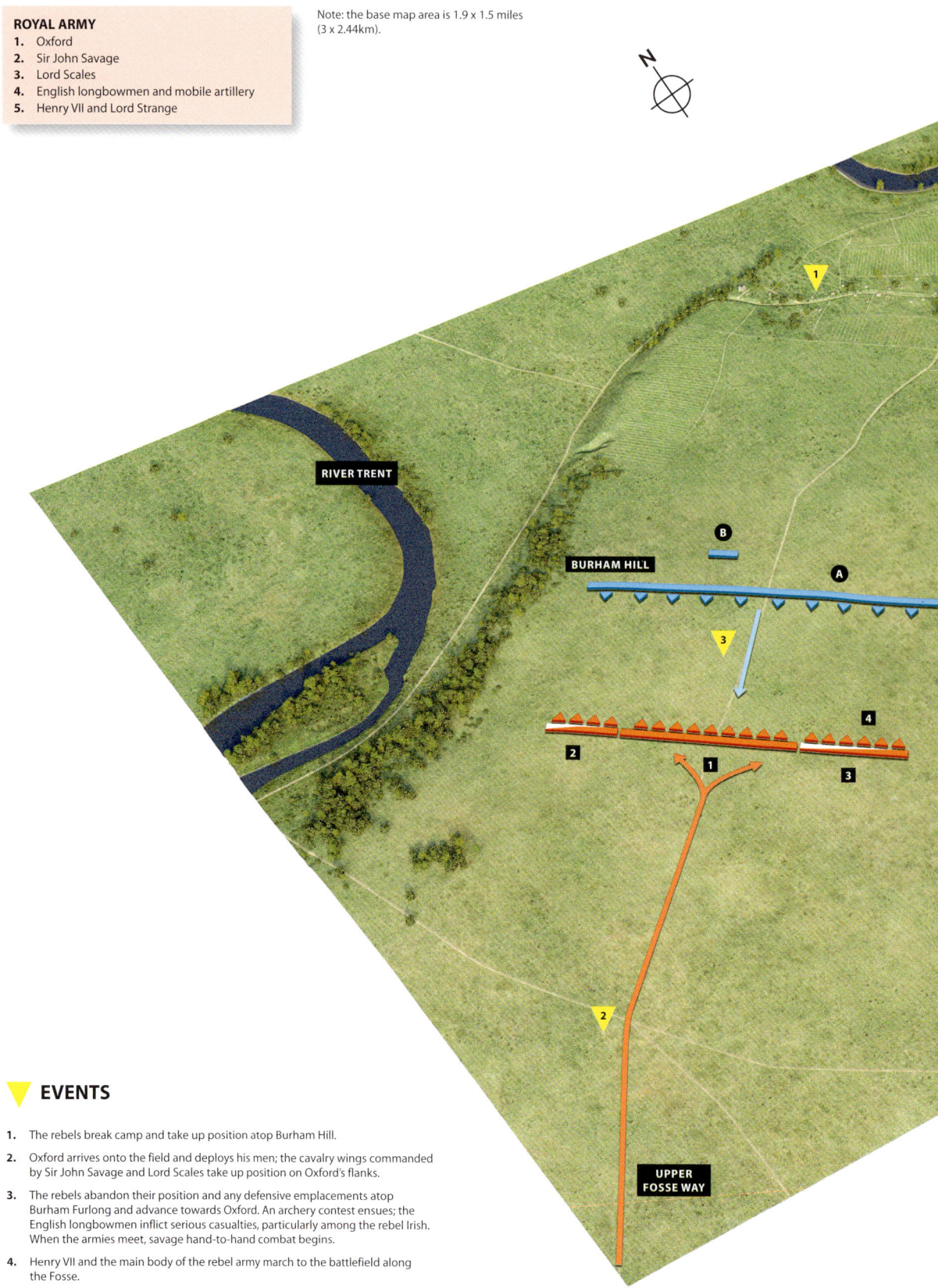

### EVENTS

1. The rebels break camp and take up position atop Burham Hill.

2. Oxford arrives onto the field and deploys his men; the cavalry wings commanded by Sir John Savage and Lord Scales take up position on Oxford's flanks.

3. The rebels abandon their position and any defensive emplacements atop Burham Furlong and advance towards Oxford. An archery contest ensues; the English longbowmen inflict serious casualties, particularly among the rebel Irish. When the armies meet, savage hand-to-hand combat begins.

4. Henry VII and the main body of the rebel army march to the battlefield along the Fosse.

# THE BATTLE COMMENCES

Oxford arrives onto the battlefield, probably marching along the Upper Fosse, and deploys his men. Lincoln, realizing that Oxford has arrived in advance of Henry VII's own battle, moves into the arrow storm unleashed by the royal vanguard. Meanwhile, Henry and the rest of the royal army march along the Fosse Way towards the battlefield.

**REBEL ARMY**
A. The rebels' single battle including Lincoln, Lovell, Schwartz and other leaders
B. Small unit guarding 'King Edward'
C. Irish archers, mercenary crossbowmen and mobile artillery

The Battle of Shrewsbury depicted in the *Beauchamp Pageant*, written and illustrated between 1483 and 1492. It shows an archery contest in the foreground, with billmen and cavalry. (Author's collection)

time needed for an archer to reload his bow meant that several waves of arrows would have taken flight before the first wave hit. To those on the receiving end, the sound of thousands of missiles hitting and ricocheting off metal would have been briefly interspersed by a moment of quiet between volleys, and then the process would repeat in a deadly rhythmic cycle.

Many battles during the Wars of the Roses showed the continuing relevance and effectiveness of these tactics. Jean de Bueil was not the only military leader who recognized that marching towards a stationary opponent put an army at a disadvantage, but even experienced battlefield commanders on the wrong end of the archery storm could find themselves with little choice other than to advance. Although plate armour was proof against most arrows, a lucky shot could always find a less armoured or exposed point of a man's body, and many were wounded and killed in this way even among the nobility. At Stoke, the more heavily armoured English and Germans would have been able to weather the storm with varying degrees of success, and the mercenary crossbowmen could shelter behind their large pavise shields, but the Irish, many of whom were lightly armoured, were decimated. Vergil says that although they conducted themselves with great courage, 'yet since in accordance with their national custom they fought with bodies unprotected by any armour, they fell more than anybody else, and their slaughter was a great source of fear to the others'. Drawing upon well-penned literary convention, Molinet says that they were 'shot through full of arrows like hedgehogs', and Hall echoes this in even more brutal language when he describes how they 'were stryken downe and slayne lyke dull and brute beastes'.

Those with experience of English longbow tactics may have urged them to take defensive measures beforehand. At Montlhéry (1465), Philip de Commines says that several Burgundian archers 'possessed themselves of a house, and unhinging two or three of the doors, made use of them, instead of shields'. Even if such improvised measures were taken by the Irish, there is no cause to substantially doubt the sources when they say the Irish suffered disproportionately compared to others within the rebel army. The sounds of men screaming, crying out and falling around them must have been terrible. The rebel leaders, however, had no choice but to overcome this hellish noise and exhort their men forward, doggedly, pace-by-pace, towards Oxford's front line.

### *Opening of the battle*

Although the rebels had English longbowmen, Irish bowmen, mercenary crossbowmen and arquebusiers in their ranks, they were still likely at a severe disadvantage. The lack of English recruits on their march to their battle must have resulted in a smaller number of longbowmen within their army than their enemy. Although the crossbow was an extremely effective and deadly weapon, having an even longer range than the longbow due to its massive 1,000lb draw weight, a competent archer might have loosed six arrows by the time a crossbowman had shot and reloaded his weapon. The primitive handguns carried in the Wars of the Roses had a maximum range of $c.$590ft (180m), but were difficult and time-consuming to load, meaning that in practice they were often fired within 65ft (20m) of the enemy. The Irish bowmen, while skilful, wielded bows that were substantially smaller and less powerful than the English equivalent. As they moved forward, the rebels would have returned fire as best they could, no doubt causing casualties, but the march forward inevitably made shooting and reloading more difficult than for their stationary opponents.

Whether the arrow storm forced the rebels to move or they willingly advanced to engage the enemy, the army needed to march forward in unison to maintain its cohesion. The German mercenaries relied on their solid formations to effectively use their pikes and halberds, and their position and discipline within the front rank must have encouraged all those who followed behind. As they moved forward, sections of the army might have had to halt on occasion so that the line remained unified.

In the last few metres before the armies clashed there would have been a flurry of activity. Oxford's archers would have retreated behind the lines of billmen and men-at-arms to act as sharpshooters and supporting troops, armed with swords and bucklers. The surviving Irish kerns and galloglass attendants would have darted in front of their fellows to throw their javelins. Perhaps most lethal were the handguns of the German mercenaries, which at short range could easily pierce through plate armour and cause gaps to form in the enemy line.

The viciousness of the guns was matched by the ferocity of the hand-to-hand fighting when the armies met. In the November parliament of 1487, the weapons used by the rebels were listed as 'swords, spears, morris-pike, bows [and] guns', each of which were now used to deadly effect. The force of the attack is hinted at by André, who says that at a certain point, the rebels thought they had overcome their enemies. Oxford, however, managed to hold his men together, and the battle devolved into a brutal blow-for-blow exchange. Vergil praises both sides for fighting 'boldly and bitterly' and says that the 'Germans in the forefront, rough men and exercised in arms did not yield to the English' and 'fought on equal terms for more than three hours'. The *York House Book* does not describe the action in detail, but agrees that 'there was a soore batell'. Otherwise, the sources are silent about the ebb and flow of the encounter.

In part, this must be a result of the general chaos of battle, which made it difficult for combatants and observers to know exactly what was happening. Once the armies had closed, the opportunity to employ tactics or direct men was extremely limited. Each man was forced to fight for his life and those of his nearest companions amid a swirling sea of chaos and violence, without any awareness of what was happening elsewhere on the battlefield. Within this maelstrom, the household men and retainers surrounding their lord would experience particularly fierce action as their enemies did all they could to slay their leader and his standard-bearer. The ferocity of hand-to-hand combat and the effect of sharp and concussive weapons in these situations could be extreme, as battlefield graves of the period vividly demonstrate. Perversely, these dangers inspired some combatants to individual acts of self-sacrifice and feats of arms, as described in *Le Jouvencel*:

> What a joyous thing is war, for many fine deeds are heard and seen in its course, and many good lessons learnt from it ... You love your comrade so much in war. When you see that your quarrel is just and your blood is fighting well, tears rise in your eyes. A great sweet feeling of loyalty and pity fills your heart on seeing

**JOHN DE LA POLE, EARL OF LINCOLN, FIGHTS FOR HIS LIFE, BATTLE OF STOKE, 16 JUNE 1487 (PP.76–77)**

John de la Pole, Earl of Lincoln (1), fights for his life as his army is cut down around him; the Irish contingent in their distinctive yellow clothing (2), and the German-Swiss mercenaries wielding their long pikes (3). Francis Lovell's banner can be seen behind him in the thick of the action (4), while advancing against them as part of Henry VII's vanguard, commanded by the Earl of Oxford, can be seen John Paston III (5), who would be among those knighted by a grateful king after their victory.

your friend so valiantly exposing his body to execute and accomplish the command of our Creator. And then you prepare to go and live or die with him, and for love not to abandon him. And out of that there arises such a delectation, that he who has not tasted it is not fit to say what a delight is. Do you think that a man who does that fears death? Not at all, for he feels strengthened, he is so elated, that he does not know where he is. Truly he is afraid of nothing.

We might suspect that Jean de Bueil's attitudes were unusual and reflect an elite knightly mindset not shared by others. Still, the psychological effect of fighting men rallied together around their lord or banner was highly important. At Bosworth, Vergil says that Oxford, 'afraid that in the fighting his men would be surrounded by the multitude, gave out the order through the ranks that no soldier should go more than ten feet from the standards'. This helped to rally the men and ensured they kept a close formation, allowing them to counter-attack to great effect. Considering he faced superior numbers at Stoke, it is likely that Oxford repeated these orders once again.

Vergil's description of the hand-to-hand combat lasting three hours is almost certainly exaggerated, but if the melee did go on for some time, it was probably interrupted by short pauses. These enabled men to catch their breaths and for the leaders to briefly retire from the front line to take some refreshment and assess the action. As battles progressed, piles of bodies and injured men could also cause problems, effectively creating barriers that men had to negotiate to find free ground to fight upon. These factors would have resulted in a degree of fluidity across the line of combat, but could also serve to slow the impetus of an attack. As time went by, it must have become clear that the onslaught launched by the rebels had failed to break the royal vanguard as they had hoped.

Throughout these events, there is little indication of where the rest of Henry's army was located. Probably, his slower, mostly dismounted contingent was still marching towards the battlefield. When he encountered the enemy, Oxford must have sent messengers to the king to let him know that battle would soon be joined. This would have caused the king to urge his men to march faster and soon they may even have begun to hear and catch glimpses of the battle taking place. Henry and his mounted household knights probably ventured ahead with Bedford and the other commanders to view the ongoing situation for themselves. Vergil certainly suggests the king was on the field and it is also possible that Henry's battle arrived while the battle still raged and began to gather into formation. If the battle did last for three hours as Vergil suggests, it is certainly difficult to understand how the king could have failed to arrive. If the rest of Henry's battle did reach the battlefield in time, the psychological impact on the rebels must have been severe.

With the rebel advance stalled and the possible arrival of the king's battle on the field, Oxford led a counter-attack, perhaps in the 'array triangle' he reportedly formed at Bosworth. This was the arrangement of his household men and retainers into one or more wedges, which would then drive themselves into the enemy line to force it apart. Such

A view from the top of Burham Furlong towards Newark. On a clear day, the tower of St Mary Magdalene's in Newark (over 4 miles distant) can easily be seen. (Author's collection)

**ROYAL ARMY**
1. Oxford
2. Sir John Savage
3. Lord Scales
4. Henry VII, Bedford and the king's mounted bodyguard
5. Henry's main battle
6. Lord Strange and the rearguard

Note: the base map area is 1.9 x 1.5 miles (3 x 2.44km).

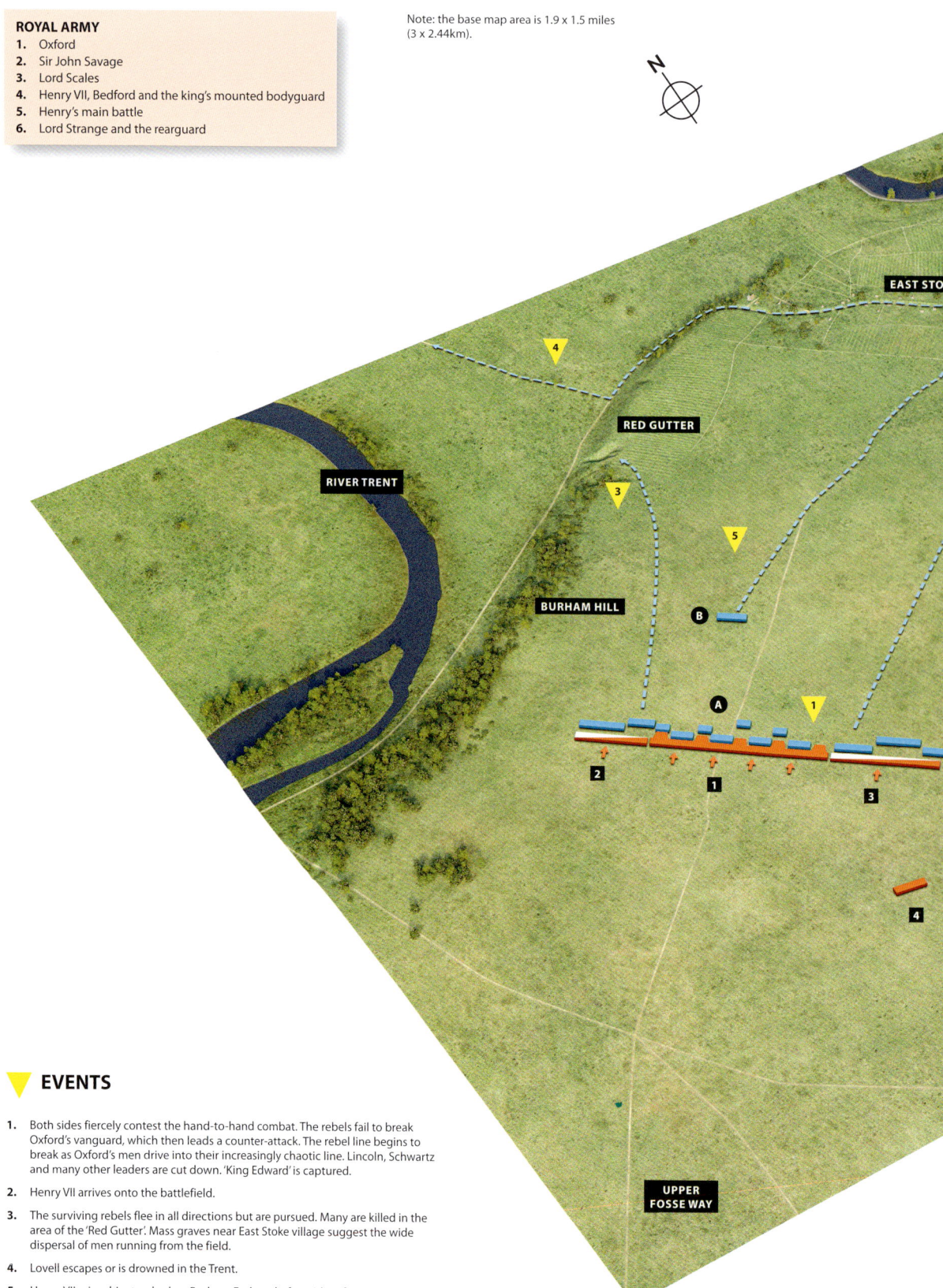

## ▼ EVENTS

1. Both sides fiercely contest the hand-to-hand combat. The rebels fail to break Oxford's vanguard, which then leads a counter-attack. The rebel line begins to break as Oxford's men drive into their increasingly chaotic line. Lincoln, Schwartz and many other leaders are cut down. 'King Edward' is captured.

2. Henry VII arrives onto the battlefield.

3. The surviving rebels flee in all directions but are pursued. Many are killed in the area of the 'Red Gutter'. Mass graves near East Stoke village suggest the wide dispersal of men running from the field.

4. Lovell escapes or is drowned in the Trent.

5. Henry VII raises his standard on Burham Furlong before riding for Newark.

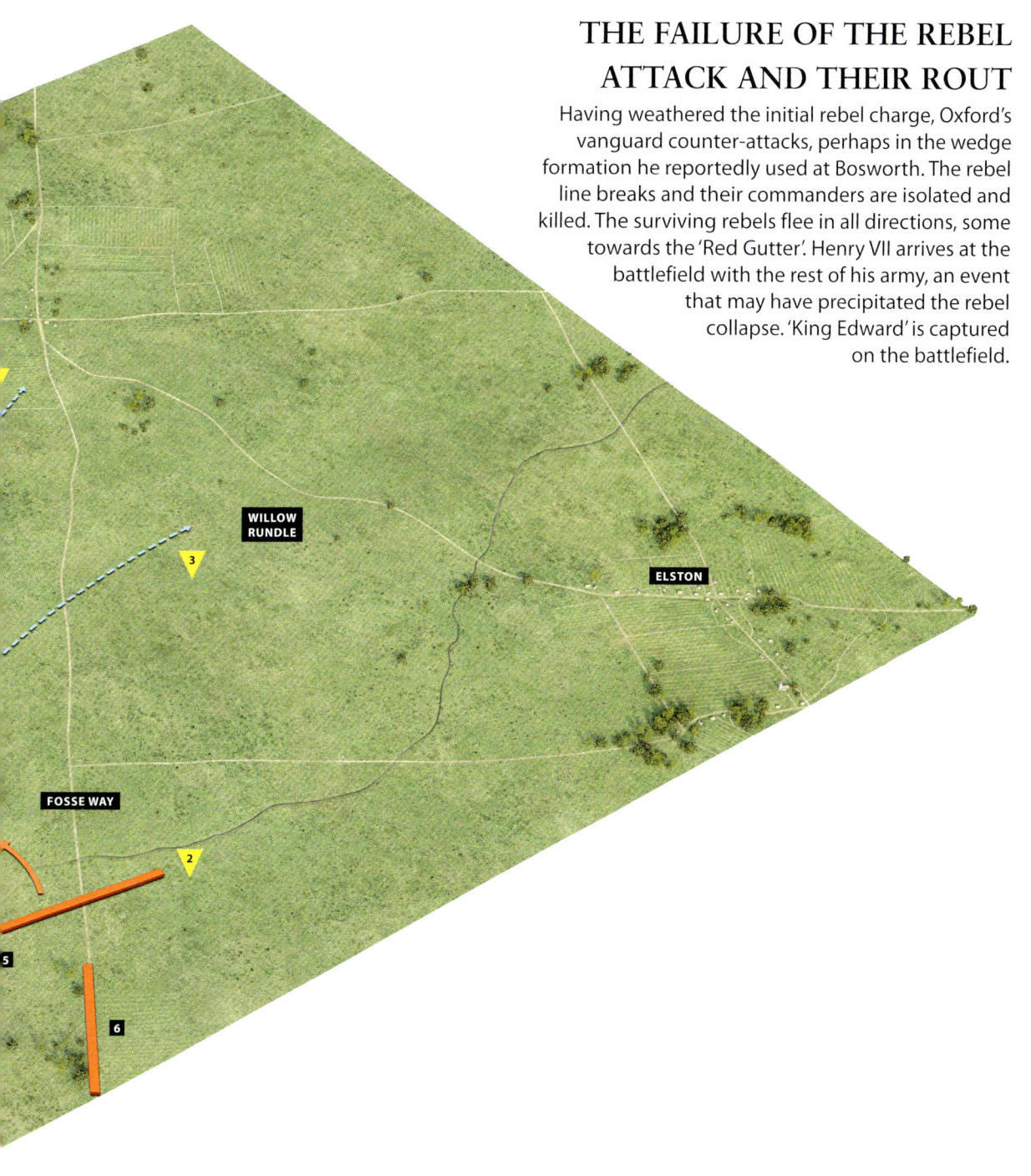

# THE FAILURE OF THE REBEL ATTACK AND THEIR ROUT

Having weathered the initial rebel charge, Oxford's vanguard counter-attacks, perhaps in the wedge formation he reportedly used at Bosworth. The rebel line breaks and their commanders are isolated and killed. The surviving rebels flee in all directions, some towards the 'Red Gutter'. Henry VII arrives at the battlefield with the rest of his army, an event that may have precipitated the rebel collapse. 'King Edward' is captured on the battlefield.

**REBEL ARMY**
A. Lincoln, Lovell, Schwartz and the other rebels
B. 'King Edward'

an opening could quickly result in a loss of cohesion among the enemy, unleashing the inherent chaos and leading to a catastrophic collapse of the entire line. André says that there rose to the sky the shout 'King Henry' and 'the blaring of trumpets on all sides', probably to signal and encourage the attack, or perhaps a result of the king's arrival on the field. Oxford then charged the enemy with such impetus, according to Vergil, 'that first it killed the opposing captains offering resistance in various places, and then put to flight the remainder, who in the course of fleeing were either captured or killed'.

## VICTORY AND DEFEAT

Vergil's account suggests that many of the rebel leaders were killed near the beginning of Oxford's attack. As men wavered, the uncertainty among the rebels would have allowed the attackers to exploit weak points, isolate individual men, and cut them down. Lincoln, Schwartz, Lovell, FitzGerald and other senior figures such as Bodrugan, Harlestone and the Harringtons would have been identifiable by the quality of their armour, the heraldry upon their surcoats and their presence near their personal standards. As the rebel battle collapsed around them, it is easily possible that the rebel leaders were rapidly overwhelmed and killed as Oxford's men surged against them. Even for the men who survived the immediate attack, few would have had the opportunity to surrender or reach their horses to escape. These were probably tethered some distance away near Burham Furlong, from where the rebels had launched their advance. Some must have been overtaken as they fled and were 'executed' on the field. Others would have fought on to the bitter end, recognizing that flight was impossible. Among these were the standard-bearers of the German mercenaries, who were expected to stand and fight until death with their standards wrapped around them to prevent their capture by the enemy. Such men had little choice but to sell their lives as dearly as they could. Meanwhile, the leaders of the vanguard, Oxford, Lord Scales and Sir John Savage, would have lost little time in ordering their men to remount their horses and give chase as soon as they saw the rout unfold. They may also have been joined by the men from the king's battle, eager and fresh after their recent arrival.

The list of the dead included the Earl of Lincoln, Martin Schwartz, Thomas FitzGerald and several of their principal knightly supporters. According to Vergil, the king had wanted Lincoln to be taken alive so that he could be questioned about the source of the conspiracy and whether there were further accomplices who 'would come to their aid at an opportune time and place'. If true, this suggests that even after the battle the king was uncertain about the extent of the conspiracy or the full list of those involved. Notwithstanding the king's orders, Vergil says that 'Henry's soldiers declined to spare him, fearing … that the sparing of a single life would destroy the lives of many'. Another success was the capture of 'King Edward' – whether Lambert Simnel or a boy called John – on the field by Robert Bellingham, an esquire of the king's household. Also captured, according to Vergil, was Richard Simons, Simnel's mentor.

The only senior rebel to escape was Francis Lovell, whose survival might hint either that he decided to retreat early enough to escape or perhaps that he was in command of a reserve behind the main line. During the battle, 'King Edward' would likely have had a small detachment of men around him, but neither this nor Lovell's contribution during the battle is mentioned by the sources. In the immediate aftermath of the battle, however, reports were circulated that Lovell had been killed, probably to emphasize the scale of Henry's victory and prevent any chance of further uprisings. Some of the Tudor chroniclers, including Vergil, took these reports at face value and said that he died on the field. However, Lovell's body was conspicuous by its absence and although it is possible that it was robbed, despoiled and buried in a mass grave without being identified, there is good reason to believe otherwise. Several contemporary sources, including the *Herald's Report*, say that he survived the battle and was 'put to flight'. On 19 June 1488, James IV of Scotland granted a safe conduct for Lovell and Sir Thomas Broughton to enter Scotland, although it is not certain they ever did so. Earlier the same year, Lovell's wife, Anne, and her mother Alice, Lady FitzHugh, still thought him alive and petitioned on his behalf. Perhaps responding to the rumour of him being in Scotland, Anne sent Lovell's associate Edward Franke north in search of him, although by February 1489, Franke had reported failure. However, in July 1491, a 'simple and poor person' of the city of York claimed to have spoken to Lovell and Broughton while he was in Scotland, although he subsequently changed his mind and provided no date for the supposed meeting.

A commemoration stone to the dead at Stoke Field located next to the tower at St Oswald's Church. (Author's collection)

By 1542, when Lovell's death was assured, Edward Hall records an alternate story, that Lovell had drowned in the Trent while crossing the river in his escape from the battlefield. Finally, in 1708, the skeleton of a man is said to have been found in a hidden room at Minster Lovell, sat at a table with a book, paper and quill pen. According to this version, Lovell returned home in secret only to die in mysterious and suspicious circumstances. A comparison can be made between this and Sir Thomas Broughton, who supposedly made his way to his old manor at Witherslack and lived the rest of his days sheltered by his erstwhile servants. Another more recent claim is that Lovell could lie buried at Gedling Church near Stoke Bardolph, one of his previous manors. In 1865, it was reported that there was an alabaster slab in the church with an effigy of a knight and an inscription (which could then still be read) giving the date 1487, meaning that it might have commemorated a knight who took part in the battle. Which of these possibilities, if any, has any truth is unclear. What is certain is that Lovell never received a pardon or had his attainder reversed. When and how he died remains a matter of speculation, but Stoke was irrefutably the last time he played any role in national affairs.

In addition to the leaders, the rout would have seen thousands of other men flee for their lives, every man for himself. They would have been pursued initially by Henry's men on foot, soon followed by those who had remounted. Such men, armed with spears, swords and battleaxes, would have found their prey exhausted by the ordeal of battle. The resulting death toll among the fleeing troops may soon therefore have exceeded the number of dead and dying already lying on the battlefield. Many would have fled back in the direction of East Stoke. Others made for the crossing over the Trent at Fiskerton, descending the escarpment via the 'Red Gutter'. Although the name of this feature might be derived from the red Keuper Marl clay that has been extracted from it since the Roman period, it is also possible it received its name from the slaughter that

The Great Hall of Minster Lovell, home of Francis Lovell. An unlikely legend records that Lovell escaped the battle and hid here until his death. (Author's collection)

took place there after the battle, similar to 'Dead Man's Bottom' at Barnet, 'Fall Ings' at Wakefield, and the 'Bloody Meadow' at Towton and Tewkesbury.

In his 1825 work *Visits to Fields of Battle in England*, Richard Brooke reported:

> Human bones, coins, and other relics indicative of a battle, have been frequently dug up ... on the south side of and within the garden of Sir Robert Bromley [*c.*575ft (175m) south of St Oswald's]. In August 1825, Sir Robert ... kindly accompanied me over part of the field of battle, and pointed out a place in his garden where many of the slain were found. They were interred in long trenches, but very few indications of armour or weapons were discovered; however, the labourers found two spurs, one of which they purloined, the other Sir Robert Bromley obtained.

In 1982, the remains of at least 11 individuals were found in a large burial pit 770ft (235m) south of the crossroads at East Stoke, next to the Fosse Way and near Deadman's Field. A part of a human skull was also found underneath the old site of the Pauncefourth Arms at East Stoke, although its date has not been evaluated.

Like the Towton grave, these burials suggest that the bodies of the dead were collected after the battle, stripped of their belongings and buried in common graves close to where they had been killed. The 11 skeletons in the Stoke burial pit were articulated (complete) but with their arms and legs intertwined, suggesting that the bodies had been unceremoniously dumped without care into the pit; a result of the sheer number of bodies to deal with and perhaps a sign of the prejudice shown against rebels and foreigners.

When the battle was done, King Henry rode to the top of Burham Furlong and raised his standard above the battlefield. There he surveyed the carnage and probably appointed captains to continue the pursuit of the rebels. Molinet says that this lasted two days and that while the surviving 200 mercenaries were allowed to depart without pay, the English and Irish were hanged. If Molinet's earlier number of 1,600 mercenaries in the rebel army is accurate, it indicates that the mortality rate at Stoke may have been exceptionally high, or perhaps only that the Germans bore the brunt of the fighting. The *Herald's Report* and Vergil give a figure of 4,000 dead and the *York House Book* 5,000. Of these, a significant number must have been Irish, killed during the battle and the aftermath. Far from home and conspicuous by their dress, hairstyles and language, very few that survived the battle can have escaped back to Ireland without being apprehended and punished.

Henry may also have stopped briefly to see for himself the dead bodies of Lincoln, Schwartz and FitzGerald. On confirming their deaths, he then

A spur said to have been found on the battlefield and traditionally associated with the events of 1487. Unfortunately, the style and decoration indicate that it is English, *c.*1610–20. (Author's collection)

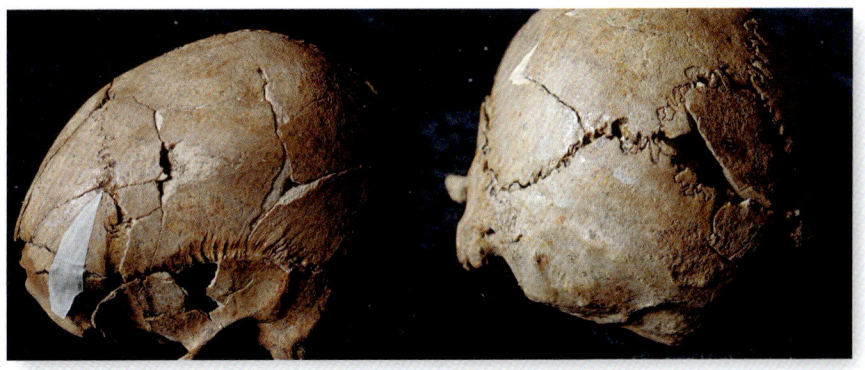

The skull of one of the 11 bodies found in the mass grave at Stoke. It displays sharp force trauma to the left parietal of the cranium (left) and the upper right of the rear of the skull (right), both injuries perhaps caused by a sword or other cutting weapon. (Caroline Sims, The National Civil War Centre – Newark Museum)

rode immediately without dismounting to Newark. There he received 200 marks from the town as a contribution and demonstration of their loyalty, before he proceeded to the Church of St Mary Magdalene to give thanks for his victory, laying one of his standards upon the altar. He had much to give thanks for. The rebellion and its leaders had been defeated or killed in battle without the loss of any significant nobleman on his side. Edward Hall says that 'not halfe of them which foughte in the forward and gave the onset [were] slayne or hurt'.

Some other possibilities exist about the fate of Lincoln and Schwartz. A Swiss account describes how Schwartz was apprehended, having been severely wounded on the battlefield, and executed on a scaffold over a river. There is also a local tradition that Lincoln and Schwartz died fighting and were buried near the site of the Willow Rundle with willow stakes driven through their bodies. A second tradition says that a dying soldier prayed to his patron saint for water on the spot and that immediately the spring gushed with fresh water.

Henry spent the evening of the battle in Newark, probably at the castle. The thanksgiving included the promotion of many more men to knighthood. The *Herald's Report* says that Henry made 70 knights and 13 bannerets, mostly after the battle was complete. Letters were soon sent around the country giving news of the king's victory. The *York House Book* records that tidings from the field arrived at the city as early as three in the morning on Sunday 17 June, whereupon the mayor, aldermen and officers went to the minster to give thanks for the victory and listen to the psalm of *Te Deum Laudamus* sung in the choir.

After leaving Newark, Henry went to Lincoln, where he dismissed the bulk of his army, arranged for a three-day thanksgiving to be celebrated and sent Christopher Urswick with his battle standard to the church at Walsingham, 'to be dedicated to God as a trophy and monument to the victory he had gained with the help of the divine Virgin'. Vergil says that several prisoners were then punished with death, although their identities are not recorded. Henry then travelled back to Kenilworth, where he rejoined his wife, his mother and perhaps his infant son.

John Paston III was knighted by King Henry VII for his part in the victory at the Battle of Stoke. (© Graham Turner www.studio88.co.uk)

# AFTERMATH

### PUNISHMENT AND REWARD

With the rebellion defeated, Henry wrote to several foreign powers informing them of his victory. On 5 July, he sent a letter to Pope Innocent VIII complaining about the Irish prelates and asking him to 'proceed against them'. He also reported that there had been violence in London when false rumours had arrived of his defeat. An obscure individual called John Swit had broken sanctuary from Westminster Abbey with other malcontents, taken up arms and begun to plunder nearby houses. He had allegedly criticized the papal bull promulgated in Henry's favour and asked 'what signify censures of church or pontiff?' On pronouncing these words, Swit had then 'instantly fell down dead upon the ground, and his face and body immediately became blacker than soot itself, and shortly afterwards emitted such a stench that no one soever could approach it'.

Henry also took the chance to reward his supporters, such as his letter sent in October to the city of Waterford, thanking them for their support and authorizing them to seize and detain rebel ships. Some supporters were rewarded with the lands of attainted rebels, such as the grant to Henry Huddlestone of much of Sir Thomas Broughton's former property. In November, the king's status and security were underlined when his wife Elizabeth received her coronation as queen in Westminster Abbey.

Just as importantly, Henry took action against surviving rebels and 28 men were attainted in the parliament that met in November 1487. The abbots and monasteries who had aided the rebel army received fines and had to sue for pardon. John Scrope, Thomas Scrope and Edmund Hastings were imprisoned and bound for large sums as security against their future good behaviour. Although they were all later released, Henry took the precaution of imposing a condition on the Scropes that they were not to travel more than 22 miles from Windsor. Henry was still distrustful enough in 1492 and 1497 to bind John and Thomas for 12,000 and 5,000 marks, respectively, in reaction to news of Perkin Warbeck's rebellion. However, neither rose in the pretender's favour. John would later fight against the Scots and helped raise the siege at Norham Castle in 1497. Thomas served Henry overseas in 1492 with one man-at-arms, 15 horses and 15 archers. Many other less prominent men who had rebelled were similarly granted pardons after a short time. With so many of the rebel leaders dead, Henry could afford to be merciful to the remainder.

The arms of Henry VII in the east window of St Mary Magdalene Church, Newark, said to commemorate Henry's visit to the church after the battle. (Author's collection)

Some rebels even went on to successful careers in Henry's service. Richard Redman, Abbot of Shap, rose through the ranks to become Bishop of Ely. Alexander Appleby entered Henry's service as a gentleman usher of the king's chamber and was granted two farms in the lordship of Penrith in August 1490. The success of Henry's lenient approach of allowing men back into favour or accommodation with the new government is demonstrated by the fact that only three former rebels continued to resist his rule. Edward Franke tried to rescue the Earl of Warwick from the Tower in 1489, which resulted in Abbot Sante of Abingdon's attainder. Rowland Robinson and Richard Harlestone entered Margaret of York's service and would go on to support Warbeck in his efforts against Tudor rule.

In Ireland, Henry also decided upon a policy of reconciliation. In January 1488, he asked for information about the prelates who had aided the rebellion and, in April, he ordered Maurice FitzGerald, Earl of Desmond, to arrest any rebels he could find. However, on 25 May 1488, Henry issued a general pardon to the 'whole commonality of the city of Dublin', including several named Irish nobles and prelates such as the Earl of Kildare. In reality, Henry had little other choice than to issue this pardon unless he was prepared to venture to Ireland himself with a significant military force.

To establish royal authority, Henry sent Sir Richard Edgcumbe to the country, with a small force of around 500 men, with authority to receive oaths of allegiance, grant pardons and give safe conducts. A detailed account of this expedition, possibly written by Edgcumbe himself, describes the meeting of Edgcumbe and Kildare as awkward and unenthusiastic. At first, the earl said he was away on pilgrimage and insisted that Edgcumbe travel to see him. In return for this break of protocol, Edgcumbe offered him none of the usual courtesies at their meeting. When presented the king's terms,

# Rebellions against Henry VII after 1487

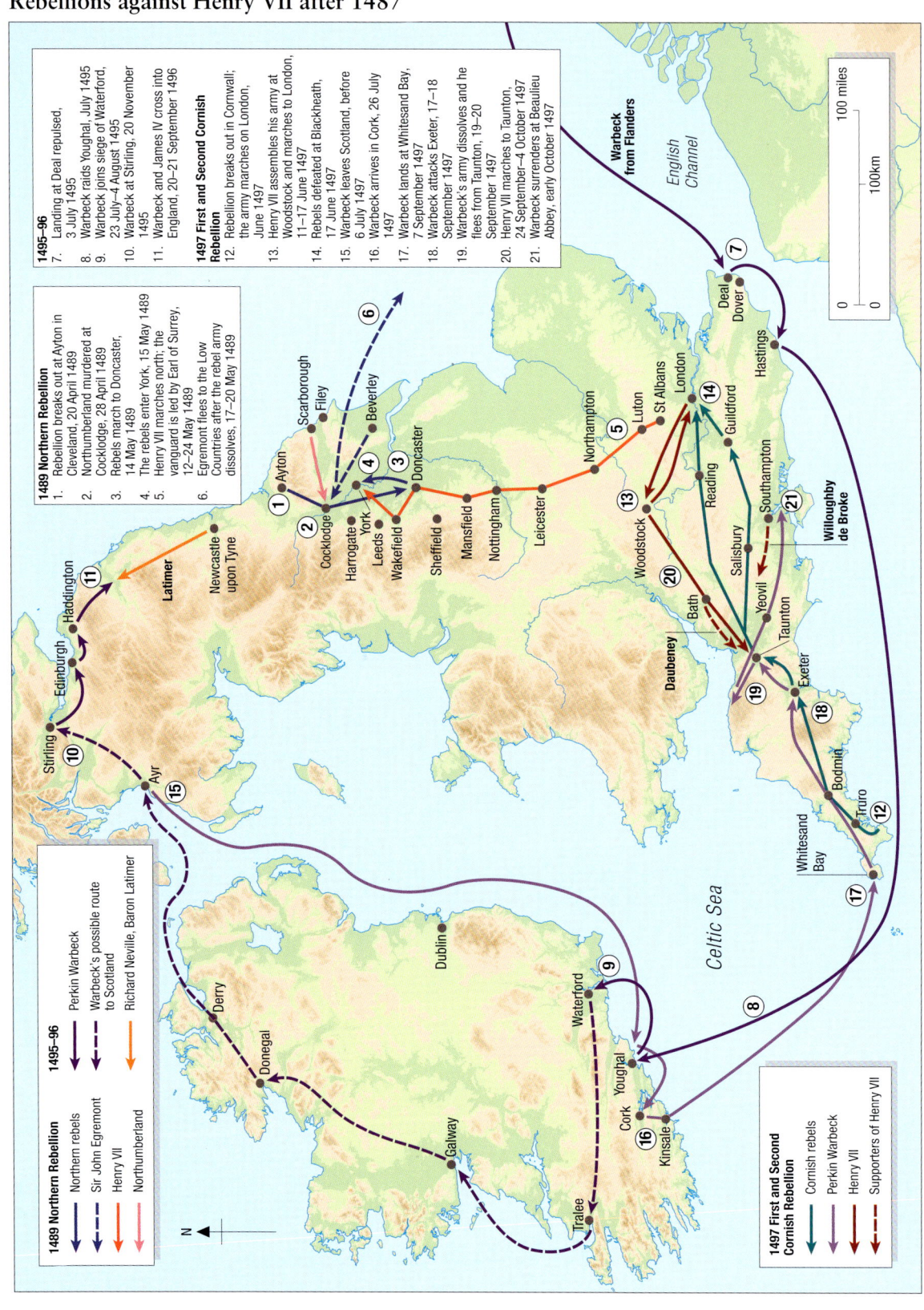

Kildare and a number of other Irish lords strongly objected to certain clauses, particularly that stipulating the forfeiture of their land should they rebel again. Eventually, an agreement was reached and Kildare swore fealty alongside Darcy of Platten and the Bishop of Meath, two other prominent men in the rebellion. Kildare was confirmed in his role as deputy lieutenant and the next day the oath was administered to the mayor of Dublin and leading citizens.

Kildare travelled to London in 1489, but according to the *Book of Howth* any awkwardness was quickly forgotten and he won over the king completely with his charisma and bravado. During a conversation between the king and the Bishop of Meath, the latter supposedly remarked to Henry that 'all Ireland cannot rule yonder gentleman', gesturing towards Kildare. 'No?' said Henry, 'then he is meet to rule all Ireland, seeing all Ireland cannot rule him.' Finally, Henry ensured that all government records of the impostor's coronation and the parliament held in his name were destroyed. No record of the rebellion was allowed to be kept that was not Henry's own.

The pretender Earl of Warwick employed in the kitchen of Henry VII in Cassell's *Illustrated History of England*, published in 1858. (Author's collection)

As for Lambert Simnel, Henry put him to work, first in the scullery and later as a falconer. The *Book of Howth* repeats this story, adding the detail that Henry later had Simnel serve a group of Irish lords to underline the folly of their actions in 1487. The Irish did not recognize the boy until Henry pointed him out, at which juncture they refused to drink from the cups Simnel had handed them. The tension was broken only when the Lord of Howth decided to drain his cup, 'for the wine's sake and mine own sake also; and for thee [Simnel], as thou art, so I leave thee, a poor innocent.' The same day, Henry is supposed to have made another pointed joke at the expense of his guests, remarking, 'My masters of Ireland, you will crown apes at length', a pointed reference to Simnel's coronation and Kildare's heraldic supporter. Simnel's later life is shrouded in mystery. In 1525, he was granted robes at the funeral of Sir Thomas Lovell, a counsellor of Henry VII who had fought at Stoke. In 1534 he was still alive and is mentioned in Vergil's *Anglica Historia*, published the same year, but afterwards he disappears from the historical record.

# FURTHER PLOTS

In 1489, a short-lived rebellion arose from the efforts of the Earl of Northumberland to collect a new tax granted by parliament to Henry VII

Perkin Warbeck drawn in the *Recueil d'Arras*, a mid-16th-century manuscript sometimes attributed to the Netherlandish artist Jacques Le Boucq. (Arras, Bibliothèque Municipale, ms. 266, fol. 23r)

to help support Brittany against France. Northumberland reacted to a gathering in Cleveland, but when he met it at Cocklodge, near Thirsk, he was assassinated – the only person killed in the entire rising. Although Vergil and the *Great Chronicle of London* mention the rebel's sympathy with potential Yorkist rivals to Henry VII, the only noble leader co-opted into joining was Sir John Egremont, a distant relative of Northumberland. According to the Paston Letters, the rebels associated themselves with St Thomas Becket, probably on account of his commonly held resistance to Henry II's plans for taxes on the poor.

Henry VII's and his nobilities' horror of Northumberland's murder by the rabble – abandoned by his retinue and 'those to whom he gave fees and was right special lord' – caused a predictably severe reaction. A large army was hastily assembled with an advance under Thomas Howard, Earl of Surrey. Meanwhile, the rebels had broken into York and taken up quarters in the city. However, by the time Henry VII arrived, the rebellion had collapsed and little further action was necessary other than the execution of Robert Chambers of Ayton, an early leader of the rebellion, and several other prominent instigators. Surrey was left in the North, where he proved competent in the re-establishment of order and the healing of wounds in the region.

In 1491, the next serious threat to Henry VII emerged in the person of Perkin Warbeck, a cloth trader from Tournai. While visiting Cork in December 1491 to sell silk, he was prevailed upon by Yorkist partisans to claim to be Richard of York, the younger of the two princes who had disappeared in the Tower, based upon his supposed close resemblance to the royal prince. Warbeck gained the backing of the Earl of Desmond and later Charles VIII of France. Charles' use for him ended when Henry secured a treaty between France and Brittany that also specified that Warbeck should receive no support or safe conduct. Warbeck and his adherents escaped and made their way to the court of Margaret of York. Henry suspended trade with the Low Countries in an attempt to force Margaret to disown Warbeck, but this proved counter-productive and Warbeck was sent on to Vienna to meet and win the support of Maximilian of Austria.

Warbeck accompanied Maximilian back to the Low Countries in 1494, but the conspiracy suffered a blow when one of their English partisans, Sir Robert Clifford, defected back to Henry VII, resulting in the arrest and execution of several plotters, most significantly William Stanley, brother to the Earl of Derby. On 3 July 1495, Warbeck sailed to England with ships and men supplied by Maximilian and Margaret, but an attempted landing at Deal on 3 July failed. An advance landing party was overwhelmed by local recruits, with 163 men captured and around 150 killed. Warbeck and most of his men were forced to watch impotently from their ships before abandoning the captured men and setting sail to Ireland. At Waterford, his supporters joined Desmond in his siege of the city. When this failed, Warbeck soon found yet another patron in James IV of Scotland. On 20 November, he was welcomed to Stirling Castle despite an official truce between James and Henry. On 21 September 1496, James and Warbeck invaded England, the latter having promised to hand over the border stronghold of Berwick in return for Scottish support. Warbeck almost immediately withdrew from the campaign, discouraged by the lack of enthusiasm he received from the local English inhabitants. James was left to demolish a few towers before he too retreated as an English armed force under Lord Latimer advanced north towards him.

In May 1497, another opportunity arose for Warbeck when Henry's heavy taxation and political mishandling caused a rebellion in Cornwall. Led by Thomas Flamank, a Cornish gentleman, Michael Joseph An Gof, a blacksmith, and later the impoverished noble Lord Audley, the rebels marched on London, apparently calling on Warbeck to join them. The rebellion was crushed by Henry VII and Oxford at Blackheath on 17 June. Warbeck landed in Cornwall by way of Ireland two months later on 7 September. He had received little support in Ireland, but when he reached Cornwall, his forces grew quickly, reportedly reaching up to 8,000 men. Warbeck laid siege to Exeter on 17 September, but the Earl of Devon and his garrison stoutly defended the city against them and forced the rebels to withdraw to Taunton. Caught in a pincer between Giles, Lord Daubeney, advancing from the north and Robert, Lord Willoughby de Broke, moving from Portsmouth, the rebel army began to melt away until, in the early hours of 21 September, Warbeck and his closest supporters made their escape. He took sanctuary at Beaulieu Abbey, Hampshire, but was recognized and surrendered on promise of pardon. Brought before Henry at Taunton Castle on 5 October, Warbeck confessed his identity as an impostor.

Paraded through London and then taken with the king on progress, Warbeck escaped, only to be recaptured, displayed in the stocks and then locked in shackles in the Tower. In 1499, he was entangled in a plot to free Edward, Earl of Warwick, and himself from imprisonment. Warbeck was hanged at Tyburn on 23 November 1499 after delivering a final public confession of being an impostor. Warwick, whose existence had threatened Henry for so long, was beheaded on Tower Hill five days later. Earlier in 1499, another impostor who claimed to be Warwick, in reality, a cordwainer from London called Ralph Wilford, was hanged on Old Kent Road.

Although there would be other threats to Henry's rule, he would die in his bed on 21 April 1509, amassing enormous wealth and achieving a political dominance over the nobility unknown to most of his predecessors. Even so, the threat of the Yorkist claimants never fully left him or his son, Henry VIII. Most dangerous were the brothers of John de la Pole, Earl of Lincoln. It was not until 1539 that the last of these, William de la Pole, died in the Tower after being kept imprisoned for 37 years, longer than any other prisoner in its history.

# THE BATTLEFIELD TODAY

Today, the battlefield can be explored effectively on foot. A new battlefield walk was created in 2018 through a partnership between Nottinghamshire County Council and the Battlefields Trust featuring five interpretation panels. This walk crosses open working farmland and uses a mixture of public bridleways, footpaths and metalled roads and pavements. The trail should take approximately one and a half hours to complete. It offers good views of the generally accepted location of the battlefield and the possible deployments of the royal and rebel armies.

The starting point for the battlefield walk is on Trent Lane, across a roundabout from Eden Hall Day Spa. Parking can be found in two laybys located on either side of the Fosse Way about 656–1,312ft (200–400m) from the roundabout. From this point, the sloping character of the terrain up to Burham Furlong can be appreciated. The first display panel on the walk provides some historical background to the battle. Ten minutes' walk up the lane you will reach another track called Humber Lane, running along the same course as the Upper Fosse Way. The road is now private land and there may be working farm machinery using it for access. The area around the meeting point of the two lanes is probably close to where the two armies met in hand-to-hand combat. The second panel is located nearby and discusses how the battle was fought.

The walk then continues along Trent Lane. To the north, the hill of Burham Furlong, where the rebels began the battle, can be viewed and appreciated. The lane then descends steeply down the escarpment to the north of the battlefield. At the bottom, turn right and follow the line of the ridge. Near the 'Red Gutter', another interpretation panel discusses the end of the battle. Unfortunately, the 'Red Gutter' itself is private and considerably overgrown. Carrying on the path, walkers can turn left towards Fiskerton, the likely river crossing of the rebels, or carry on straight towards the church. A fourth panel shortly before this discusses the burial of the dead after the battle. In the tower of St Oswald's, an exhibition can be found on the battle, made up of the detailed display panels from the previous commemorations and battlefield walk created in 1987. On Church Lane, the archaeological remains of the East Stoke village, once considerably larger than its present size, can be seen in the field south of the road. The final display panel, which gives information about the medieval village, can be found near the crossroads over the Fosse Way. On the way back to the layby, walkers can take a quick detour down Elston Lane. Near the end of the road near the new A46, the old location of the Willow Rundle Spring can be found, which local folklore connects to the events of the battle.

The nearby historic market town of Newark has several landmarks connected to the battle. Chief among these are Newark Castle and the Church of St Mary Magdalene, both of which were visited by Henry VII after he had secured victory. The National Civil War Centre – Newark Museum features excellent displays about the history of the town, including one of the skulls found during excavations of a burial pit close to East Stoke. Slightly farther afield is Southwell Minster, past which the rebels marched on the day before the battle. Nottingham is sadly much changed since 1487, although some remains of the medieval castle still exist.

Excellent displays of medieval arms and armour can be seen in the Royal Armouries Museum in Leeds. Stoke is also within an hour's drive from the site of Bosworth Field, the preceding battle during the Wars of the Roses. The Bosworth Heritage Centre has an excellent exhibition that provides information on all aspects of 15th-century warfare, together with hands-on experiences. There are also archaeological finds from the battlefield, all of which are directly comparable to the equipment and artefacts soldiers would have carried at Stoke.

One of the interpretation panels on the battlefield walk. (Author's collection)

# SELECT BIBLIOGRAPHY

*Primary Sources*

'A short and a brief memory ... of the first progress of our sovereign lord Henry the Seventh' in Leland, J., *Collectanea*, Vol IV, ed. Hearne, T., Oxford (1774)
*Bacon: The History of the Reign of King Henry the Seventh*, ed. Vickers, B., Cambridge University Press: Cambridge (1994)
Bernard André, 'Vita Henrici Septimi' in *Memorials of King Henry the Seventh*, ed. Gairdner, J., London (1858)
*Book of Howth* in *Calendar of Carew Manuscripts*, Vol. V, ed. Brewer, J.S. & Bullen, W., London (1871)
*Chroniques de Jean Molinet, 1474–1506*, ed. Doutrepont, G. & Jodogne, O., 3 vols, Brussels (1935–37)
*Hall's Chronicle containing the History of England*, ed. Ellis, H., London (1809)
*Letters and Papers Illustrative of the Reigns of Richard III and Henry VII*, ed. Gairdner, J., 2 vols, London (1861–63)
*Letters and Papers, Foreign and Domestic, Henry VIII, Volume 4, 1524–1530*, ed. Brewer, J.S., London (1875)
*Letters of the kings of England*, ed. Halliwell-Phillipps, J.O., London (1848)
*Materials for a History of the Reign of Henry the Seventh*, ed. Campbell, W., 2 vols, London (1873–77)
*Paston Letters and Papers of the Fifteenth Century*, ed. Davis, N., Oxford University Press: Oxford (1971–76)
*The Anglica Historia of Polydore Vergil: A.D. 1485–1537*, ed. Hay, D., Royal Historical Society: London (1950)
*The antiquities and history of Ireland*, James Ware, Dublin (1705)
*The Croyland Chronicle Continuations, 1459–1486*, eds. Pronay, N. & Cox, J., Sutton Publishing: London (1986)
*The Great Chronicle of London*, eds. Thomas, A.H. & Thornley, I.D., London (1938)
*The Plumpton Letters and Papers*, ed. Kirby, J., Cambridge University Press: Cambridge (1996)
*The Reign of Henry VII from Contemporary Sources*, ed. Pollard, A.F., 3 vols, Longmans: London (1913–14)
*Tudor Royal Proclamations*, ed. Hughes, P.L & Larkin, J.F., Vol I, Yale University Press: London (1964)
*York House Books 1461–1490*, ed. Attreed, L.C., 2 vols, Alan Sutton: Stroud (1991)

*Secondary Sources*

Baldwin, D., *Stoke Field: The Last Battle of the Wars of the Roses*, Pen & Sword: Barnsley (2006)
Bartlett, T. & Jeffery, K., *A Military History of Ireland*, Cambridge University Press: Cambridge (2008)
Bennett, M., *Lambert Simnel and the Battle of Stoke*, St Martin's Press: New York (1987)
Bennett, M., 'Henry VII and the Northern Rising of 1489' in *The English Historical Review*, Vol. 105, No. 414 (1990), pp. 34–59
Boardman, A.W., *The Medieval Soldier in the Wars of the Roses*, Alan Sutton: Stroud (1998)
Brooke, R., *Visits to Fields of Battle, in England, of the Fifteenth Century*, London (1858)
Brown, C., *A History of Newark-on-Trent; Being the Life Story of an Ancient Town*, 2 vols, Newark (1904–07)
Cannan, F., *Galloglass 1250–1600: Gaelic Mercenary Warrior*, Osprey: Oxford (2010)
Chrimes, S.B., *Henry VII*, Yale University Press: London (1999)
Croker, T. Crofton, *The Popular Songs of Ireland*, Henry Colburn: London (1839)
Cunningham, S., *Henry VII*, Routledge: London (2007)
Fletcher, A., & Macculloch, D., *Tudor Rebellions*, Routledge (2016)
Gravett, C., *Bosworth 1485: The Downfall of Richard III*, Osprey: Oxford (2021)
Jones, M.K., & Underwood, M.G., *The King's Mother Lady Margaret Beaufort, Countess of Richmond and Derby*, Cambridge University Press: Cambridge (1992)
Jones, R., 'Janico Markys, Dublin, and the coronation of "Edward VI" in 1487' & 'The Book of Howth's account of the Lambert Simnel conspiracy: an eyewitness account?' in *Medieval Dublin*, Vol. 14 & 17 (2012–19)
Langley, P., *The Princes in the Tower: Solving History's Greatest Cold Case*, History Press: Stroud (2023)
Luckett, D.A., 'The Thames Valley Conspiracies against Henry VII' in *Historical Research*, Vol. 68, No. 166 (1995), pp. 164–72.
Martin, F.X., 'The Crowning of a King at Dublin, 24 May 1487' in *Hermathena*, No. 144 (1988), pp. 7–34
Miller, D., *The Swiss at War*, Osprey: Oxford (1995)
Nicholls, K., *Gaelic and Gaelicized Ireland in the Middle Ages*, Lilliput Press: Dublin (2003)
Otway-Ruthven, A.J., *A History of Medieval Ireland*, New York (1993)
Pugh, T.B., 'Henry VII and the Tudor Nobility' in Bernard, G.W., ed., *The Tudor Nobility*, Manchester University Press: Manchester (1992)
Richards, J., *Landsknecht Soldier 1486–1560*, Osprey: Oxford (2002)
Ross, J., *John de Vere, Thirteenth Earl of Oxford (1442–1513): 'The Foremost Man of the Kingdom'*, Boydell Press: Woodbridge (2011)
Strickland, M. & Hardy, R., *The Great Warbow*, Sutton Publishing: Stroud (2005)
Williams, C.H., 'The Rebellion of Humphrey Stafford in 1486' in *The English Historical Review*, Vol. 43, No. 170 (1928), pp. 181–9
Wroe, A., *Perkin: A Story of Deception*, Vintage (2004)

*Online*

Individual biographies can be found on the Oxford Dictionary of National Biography website at: https://www.oxforddnb.com/
The Richard III Society has published many articles online at: http://www.richardiii.net

# INDEX

Figures in **bold** refer to illustrations.

Abingdon 12, 26, 58, 87
André, Bernard 14–15, 19, 27, 61, 64, 70, 71, 75, 82
archers 29–30, 50, 63, 67, 71, **72**, **73**, 74–75, 86
armour 5, **22**, **26**, 30–32, **33**, **34**, 35, 55, 60, 64, 67, 74–75, 82, 84, 93
artillery 30, 33, 46, 63, **72**, **73**
attainder 7, 13, **25**, 37, 59, 61, 83, 87
Austria 26, 30–31, 90
axes 30, 33, 35, 83

battles:
    Battle of Barnet **4**, 17, 19, 22–23, 25, 84
    Battle of Blore Heath **4**, 62–63
    Battle of Bosworth **4**, 5–6, 7, 8, 9, 17, 20–29, **30**, 37, 39–41, 45, 51, 55–56, 58, 65, 67, 79, **81**, 93
    Battle of Edgcote **4**, 19, 21
    Battle of Hexham **4**, 27
    Battle of Northampton **4**, 27, 63
    Battle of St Albans **4**, 22
    Battle of Tewkesbury **4**, 17, 21, 23, 84
    Battle of Towton **4**, 17, 27, 65, 84
    Battle of Wakefield **4**, 41, 84
Beaufort, John (Duke of Somerset) **18**, 19
Beaufort, Margaret 7, **18**, 19, **20**, 21, 24–25
Beaumont, John 15, **38**, 40
Bedingfield, Sir Edmund 29, 36, 46, 70
Bodrugan, Sir Henry 15, **38**, 40, 42, 82
Bootham Bar 17, **38**, 46, **54**, 55
bows 21, 33, 35–36, 56, 67, 71, 74–75
Bray, Sir Reginald 7, **21**, 47
Brittany 5, 17, **20**, 21, 23, 40, 90
Broughton, Sir Thomas 11, 27, 49, 62, 70, 83, 86
Broughton Tower 27, 49
Burgundian Wars 26, 31
Burgundy **16**, 17, 39, 45
Burgundy, Charles Duke of (Charles the Bold) 14, **16**, 31
Burham Furlong 60, 62, 64, 67, **71**, **72**, 79, 80, 82, 84, 92
Burham Hill 62, **66**, **72**, 80
Bury St Edmunds 29, 36, **38**, 45
Butler, Thomas (Earl of Ormond) 39, 42, 44, 47

cavalry 31–32, 48, 56, 63, 65, 67, **72**, 74
Charles VIII, King 9, 20, 90
Cheney, Sir John 29, **30**, 55, 60
Cheshire 23, 45, 58
Clarence, George (Duke of Clarence) 14–16, **18**, **22**, 37, 39, 42
Cleveland 88, 90
Clifford, Lord 29, 35, **38**, 51, **54**, 55, 61
Cocklodge **88**, 90

Cokesey, Thomas 10, 12
Colchester 8, 9, 11, 26, **38**, 45
conspiracy 11–13, 16, 26–27, 39, 45, 49, 82, 90
Cornwall 15, 18, 22, 28, 48, **88**, 91
coronation 6–7, 9, 17, **20**, 21, 23, 25, 34, 43–44, 47, 86, 89
Courtenay, Edward (Earl of Devon) 23, 28–29, 54, 55–56, 91
Coventry 30, **38**, 46–48, 56
crossbowmen 63, **73**, 74
crossbows **31**, 32, 71, 74
*Croyland Chronicle* 6, 10–11, 21, 23

Darcy, Sir William (of Platten) **42**, 43, 89
de Bueil, Jean 67, 74, 79
de la Pole, John (Earl of Lincoln) **4**, 7, 11–13, 16–17, 24, **25**, **26**, 28, 30, 37, **38**, 39, 42–43, 45–47, 49–51, **54**, 57, 58–59, 61–62, 64, **66**, 67, 71, **73**, 78, 80, 82, 84–85, 91
de la Pole, John (Duke of Suffolk) 24, **25**, **26**, 29, 46
de Vere, John (Earl of Oxford) **4**, 6, 12, 20–21, **22**, 28–30, 36, 40–41, **45**, 46, 55–56, **57**, 60–61, 65, **66**, 67, 70, 71, **72**, **73**, 74–75, 78, 79, 80, **81**, 82, 91
Devon 15, 20, **40**, 48
Doncaster 8, 16–17, **38**, 51, **57**, 58–59, 67, 88
Dublin 17, 32, **38**, 39, 41, **42**, 43, **44**, 87, **88**, 89

East Anglia 22, 28, 36, 45–46
East Stoke **57**, 59, **60**, 61–62, **66**, **73**, 80, 83–84, 92–93
Edgcumbe, Sir Richard 15, 40, 87
Edward III, King **18**, 19
Edward IV, King 6, 9, 11–12, 14–15, 17, **18**, 19–24, 26–27, 29, 30, 37, 39–41, 43–44, **65**, 71
Elston **57**, 62, **66**, **73**, 81
England 5–6, 9, 13, **16**, 17–18, 20–23, 26–27, 30, 32–33, **34**, 37, 39, 42, **44**, 47–48, 59, 63–64, 88, 90–91
Essex **22**, 30, 36, 41

Fiskerton **57**, 59, 62, **66**, 71, 83, 92
FitzGerald, Gerald (Earl of Kildare) 26, **34**, 39, 42–43, **44**, 87, 89
FitzGerald, Maurice (Earl of Desmond) 87, 90–91
FitzGerald, Thomas (of Laccagh) **4**, 13, 26, **42**, **44**, 62, 70, 82, 85
Flanders **16**, 46, 88
Flintham Lings **61**, 62
Fosse Way **57**, 59, **60**, 61–62, 64, **66**, **73**, **81**, 84, 92
Foulney Island **38**, 48
Fox, Richard (Bishop of Exeter) 6, 60
France 6, 9, 17, 20, 22–23, 29, 50, 71, 90

Franke, Edward 50, 83, 87
Furness 17, **48**, 49, 51
Furness Abbey 10, 47, **49**
Furness Fells 10, 13, 27

Gaelic 26, 32, 34, 39, 44
galloglass 32, **33**, 34–35, 63, 75
Gaunt, John of (Duke of Lancaster) **18**, 47
government 6–7, 12, 14, 16, 23, 39, 41, 47, 50, 87, 89
Grey, Thomas (Marquess of Dorset) 15, **38**, 45, 49

halberds **31**, 32–33, 36, 75
Hall, Edward 10, 21, 36, 58, 74, 83, 85
handguns **31**, 74–75
Harlestone, Sir Richard 40, 62, 82, 87
Harrington, Sir James 41, 49, 51, 62, 70, 82
Harrington, Sir Robert 41, 49, 51, 62, 82
Hastings, Sir Edmund 29, **54**, 55, 86
helmets 31, 35, **63**
Henry VI, King 16, 19, 21–23
Henry VII, King (Henry Tudor) **4**, **5**, 6, 7, 8, 9–14, **15**, **16**, 17, **18**, 19, **20**, 21, 22–30, 35, 37, **38**, 39–46, **47**, 48–49, 51, **54**, 55–56, **57**, 58–61, **65**, 67, **72**, **73**, 78, 79, 80, **81**, 82–84, 85, 86, 87, 88, 89, 90–91, 93
Henry VIII, King 17, 33, 91
herald 10, **12**, 14, **15**, 29, 44, 59–61, 64–65, 67, 82, 89
*Herald's Report* **15**, 26, 35–36, 56, 64, 67, 83–85
Herbert, William (Earl of Pembroke) 19, 21
*History of England* 27, 89
Hornby Castle 41, 49
horsemen 34–35, 56
House of Lancaster 9, 12, 56
House of York 9, 12–13, **18**, 37, 49, **54**
Howard, John (Duke of Norfolk) 22, 45, 67
Howard, Thomas (Earl of Surrey) 7, 88, 90
Humber Lane 64, 92

Ireland 9, 13–17, 23, 25–26, 32–33, **34**, 37, **38**, 39–40, 42–48, 84, 87, 89, 91

James IV, King 83, 88, 91
javelins 34–35, 75
Jervaulx Abbey 49, 50

Kenilworth Castle **38**, 46, **47**, 56, 85
kerns 33, 34–35, 51, 63–64, 75
Knaresborough 24, 41
Knight of the Garter 23–24, 27, 29

Lancashire 10, 27, 45, 48, 58
Lancaster 8, 22, 24, 28, 37

Lancastrian **11, 12**, 19, **20**, 21–22, 29, 39, 46, 65
*Landsknechte* 31–32
*Le Jouvencel* 67, 75
Leicester **8**, 30, **38**, 56, **88**
Lincoln **8**, 9, **38**, 61, 85
London 5, **8**, 12, 16, 35, **38**, 41, 45, 47, 86, **88**, 89, 91
longbowmen 63, **72**, 74
longbows 40, 71, 74
Lovell, Francis (Viscount Lovell) **4**, 8, 9, **10, 11**, 12–13, 16–17, 24–25, **26**, 27, 30, 37, 40–41, 47, 50, 58–59, 61–62, 64, 67, **73**, 78, **80**, **81**, 82–83, 84
Low Countries 9, 11, 17, 26, 31, 37, **38**, 45, 64, **88**, 90

Mancini, Dominic 65, 67, 71
Maximilian of Austria 17, 26, 30–32, 39, 90–91
Meath 34, 43–44, 89
mercenaries 26, 38, 41, 43–44, 63, **73**, 74, 84
    French mercenaries 6, 21
    German mercenaries 30–32, 35, 63–64, **70**, 74–75, **78**, 82, 84
    Swiss mercenaries 31–32, **70**, 78
Middleham 10, **11**, 49, 55
Middleham, Prince Edward of **11**, 17, 25
Milford Haven 17, 20, 23, 29
Minster Lovell 12, 26, 83, **84**
Molinet, Jean 14, 35, 39, 49, 58–59, 61, 63, 65, 67, 74, 84
Morton, Archbishop John 6, 10, 13, **14**, 15, 20, 56

Netherlands 30–31, 39
Neville, Richard (Earl of Warwick, 'the Kingmaker') 17, 22, 25
Newark **57**, 59–61, 65, **79**, **80**, 85, 87, 93
Norfolk **29**, 30, 41, 67
Nottingham **8**, 12, 25, 30, **38**, 56, 57, 58, 59, **88**, 93

Oxford **8**, 13–14, 16, **38**

pardons 7, 9–10, 12, 27, 40, 42, 44–45, 49, **50**, 83, 86–87, 91
parliament 7, 9, 28, 35, 39–40, 43, 50, 75, 86, 89
Paston, Sir John 11, 36, 47, **78**, 85
Pembroke Castle 17, **19**, 21
Percy, Henry (Earl of Northumberland) 7, 10–11, 17, 28–29, 35, **38**, 50–51, **54**, **55**, **58**, **88**, 89–90
pikemen 30–31
pikes 15, 30, **31**, 32, 63–64, 75, 78
Plantagenet, Edward (Earl of Warwick) 6, 7, **12**, 13–16, **18**, 25, 28, 37, 40, 42–43, 45, 87, 91
Plantagenet, Richard (Duke of York) **18**, 24, 39
Plunket, Edward 42, 44
Pope Innocent VIII 9, 16, 86

Princes in the Tower 14–16, 20
    Edward V 14–17, 18, 20, 24, 43, 65
    Richard, Duke of York 14–16, 18, 20, 24, 90

Radcliffe **57**, 59–61
Readeption 17, 19, 22–23
rebel army 24, 30, 32, 35–36, **51**, 56, 58, 63–65, **66**, **70**, **72**, **73**, 74, **81**, 84, 86, **88**, 91–92
rebellion 8, 9–10, **11**, 12, 16–17, 20, 22–23, 25, 27, 29, 37, **38**, 39–42, 44–47, **49**, 50, 62, 85–87, **88**, 89–91
rebels 10–12, 17, 24–25, 30, 35–37, **38**, 40–42, 44, 46–47, **48**, **49**, **50**, 51, **54**, 55, **57**, 58–59, 61, **62**, 63–65, **66**, 67, 70, 71, **72**, **73**, 74–75, **79**, **80**, **81**, 82, 84, 86–87, **88**, 90–93
'Red Gutter' **62**, **66**, **80**, **81**, 83, 92
Redhill 56, **57**
Redman, Richard (Abbot of Shap) 50, 87
Richard III, King 5–6, 7, 9, **11**, **13**, 14–15, 17, **18**, 20–25, **26**, 27–29, 30, 37, 39–42, 49, 56, 65
River Trent 22, **57**, 59, 60–62, **66**, 71, **72**, **80**, 83

sallets 32, 36, **63**
Sante, John (Abbot of Abingdon) 12–13, 16, 58, 87
Savage, Sir John **4**, 12, 23, **24**, 65, 67, **72**, **80**, 82
Schwartz, Martin 26, **27**, 32, 41, 49–50, 61, 63, **70**, **73**, **80**, **81**, 82, 84–85
Scotland 9, 17, 26, **61**, 83, **88**, 91
Scrope, John (Baron Scrope of Bolton) 17, 27, 38, 50, **51**, **54**, **55**, 86
Scrope, Thomas (Baron Scrope of Masham) 17, 27, 38, 50, **54**, **55**, 86
ships 20, 23, 30, 33, 42, 47, 86, 90–91
Simnel, Lambert (King Edward VI) 13–17, **34**, 37, **38**, 39, **42**, 43, **44**, 50, **54**, 55, 58, 62, 64, **73**, **80**, **81**, 82–83, **89**
Simons, Richard 13–15, 61, 82
Simons, William 13–15
soldiers 20, 30–34, 47–48, 60, 63, **64**, 65, 67, 71, 79, 82, 85, 93
Southwell **57**, 59, 93
spears 5, 33, 35, 75, 83
Spenser, Edmund 33, 35
St Leger, Anthony 33–34
St Oswald's Church 59, **60**, 62, 83, **84**, 92
Stafford, Henry (Duke of Buckingham) 17, 20, 23, 25, 29
Stafford, Sir Humphrey **8**, 9, **11**, 12–13, 17, 25
Stafford, Thomas 9, 11–12, 17
Stanley, George (Lord Strange) **4**, 24, 29, 35–36, **38**, **57**, 58, 67, **72**, **80**
Stanley, Thomas (Earl of Derby) 7, 12, 20, 24–25, 28, 41, 46–47, 90
Stanley, Sir Willam 17, 21, 90
Stillington, Bishop Robert 15–16
Stoke Bardolph 59, 83

swords 22, 23, 32, **33**, 35, 75, 83, **85**
Syerston **57**, **62**, **66**

Tadcaster 38, 51, 55, 67
Taite, James 11, 16
Talbot, George (Earl of Shrewsbury) **4**, **23**, 28–29, 36, **55**, **70**
Talbot, Sir Gilbert 23, 60
*The Book of Howth* 35, 44, 89
*The Great Chronicle of London* 50, 56, 61, 90
Tower of London 13–16, 20–22, 33, 49, 87, 90–91
Tudor, Edmund (Earl of Richmond) **18**, 19
Tudor, Jasper (Duke of Bedford) **4**, 7, 8, 10, 12, 17, 19, 21, **22**, **23**, 28–29, 36, 39, 41, 47, **55**, **79**, **80**
Tudor, Owen **18**, 23

Upper Fosse Way **57**, **61**, **66**, **72**, **80**, 92
Urswick, Christopher 48–49, 85

vanguard 21–22, 35–36, **55**, **59**, **61**, **65**, **66**, **67**, **70**, **73**, **78**, **79**, **80**, **81**, **82**, **88**
Vergil, Polydore 9–11, 13–14, 16, 21, 24, 27, 35, 37, 42, 48, 59, 61, 63–65, **70**, 71, 74–75, 79, 82–85, 89–90

Wales 5, 20–21, 23–24, 28, 35, 48
Wales, Prince Arthur of 12, 16–18, 25, 41, 85
Walsingham **38**, 46, 85
Warbeck, Perkin (Richard, Duke of York) 17–18, 39, 86–87, **88**, 90, 91
Wars of the Roses **4**, 11, 30, 40, 61, 63–64, 65, 67, 71, 74, 93
Waterford 41, 44, 86, **88**, 91
Welles, John (Lord Welles) 35, 58
Wensleydale **11**, 38, 49, **51**
Willoughby, Sir Robert 6, 46
Willow Rundle **66**, **81**, 85, 92
Woodville, Sir Edward (Lord Scales) **4**, 17, 23, 35, **38**, 56, **57**, 58–59, 61, 65, 67, **72**, **80**, 82
Woodville, Elizabeth 15–16, **18**, 21
Worcester **8**, 12, 38

York **8**, 9–11, 25, 27–28, 30, 34–35, 37, **38**, 46–47, 49–51, **54**, **55**, 58, 83, **88**, 90
York, Elizabeth of (Duchess of Suffolk) 24, **25**
York, Elizabeth of (Queen of England) 6, 7, 9, 12, 15, 17, **18**, 20, 23, 29, 44, 47, 56, 85–86
*York House Book* 10, 30, 35, 51, **54**, **55**, 61, 75, 84–85
York, Margaret of (Duchess of Burgundy) 8, 9, 11, 13–15, **16**, 30, **31**, 32, 37, 39–40, 42, 50, 87, 90–91
York Minster 46, **54**, 55
Yorkist 6–7, 9, 11, **12**, 20, 22–23, 25, 27, 29, 37, 39, 42, **54**, 64–65, 90–91
Yorkshire 7, 9, **11**, 41, 49–50